What's so bad about being good?

JACK R. CHRISTIANSON

SHADOW MOUNTAIN

Library of Congress Cataloging-in-Publication Data

Christianson, Jack R.
  What's so bad about being good? / Jack Christianson.
    p.   cm.
  ISBN 1-57345-819-8
  1. Christian life.   2. Christian ethics.   I. Title.
BX8656.C497   2000
248.4'89332—dc21   00-055642

Printed in the United States of America   18961-6715

10   9   8   7   6   5   4   3   2   1

For Brigham Jack

CONTENTS

Foreword

During an interview on national television, a sports announcer's final question to me was, "Steve, what most do you want to be remembered for?" The question made me stop and think for a minute. The announcer was expecting a football-related answer, but as I thought honestly about my response, I could only think of one thing. I said, "I want to be remembered for being a good man."

The definition of *good* may mean different things to different people, but I believe its meaning crosses generations and cultures in similar ways. Integrity, honesty, charity, unselfishness, service, care, and gratitude are all part of being good. The greatest thing about being good is that it is something we can choose in almost any circumstance involving people. We can opt not to hurt others. We can care for one another. We can share our time and substance. We can obey laws designed to protect others.

Being good to others is something basic that can unite all people. I am proud that I am an American, and yet as I have traveled throughout the world I have been amazed at the goodness of people in all the countries I have visited. I have observed family members, sales people, attendants, and others rushing to help loved ones or strangers in need. Good choices have a positive effect on many people, especially ourselves. As the old Chinese proverb says:

When there is righteousness in the heart,
There is beauty in the character.
When there is beauty in the character,
There will be harmony in the home.
When there is harmony in the home,
There will be order in the nation.
When there is order in the nation,
There will be peace in the world.

Some time ago while visiting a family with several children, I overheard a teenager talking about his teacher. His words impressed me. "You know what?" he asked. "If my teacher believes these things are right, they must be right because he is such a cool guy."

Recognizing that statement from a sixteen-year-old boy as the ultimate compliment, I asked the name of his teacher. He turned out to be Jack Christianson, a teacher at a local high school. Jack had played football throughout college and had had opportunities afterward to play professionally. He also had received numerous invitations to go into business. He turned down these lucrative possibilities because he wanted to help young people experience the feelings of choosing what is good. Through the years, I found out, he has taught thousands of teenagers—both in high school and college.

I soon had the privilege of meeting Jack Christianson and witnessing for myself his rapport with students. They honored and admired him because he honored and admired them. I became aware of his dedication to serving others. Jack not only teaches, writes books for young people, and gives numerous lectures, but he takes troubled children into his home, opening his door during all hours of the day and night to students in need. He brings them in, holds them, cries with them, and helps them formulate plans that make a difference in their lives. Jack travels throughout the country to promote the concept that there is nothing wrong with being good. He encourages parents to "hold on," for the worth of their children is priceless.

One exhausting experience I know of sums up the dedicated life of Jack Christianson. As an ecclesiastical leader in his church, Jack had dealt with many tragic circumstances one particular day, ending up at the hospital in the early hours of the morning to see a young girl who had attempted suicide. He came home emotionally drained with just enough time to get ready to go to work at 7:00 A.M. As his sweet wife, Melanie, witnessed his pace, she remembered a statement by a beloved church leader that had always been an inspiration to Jack: "My life is like my shoes, to be worn out in service." That afternoon Melanie purchased a much-needed pair of shoes and put them on her weary husband's pillow with a note that said, "Another pair of shoes to be worn out in the service of others."

This book is an example of Jack's service. It reaches out to all who desire goodness. Its concepts are simple and proven; they need only be tried in order to be determined good. The ability to discern good is basic to human nature, but we must act upon our inner feelings. By doing so, it will be said of us that we "went about doing good" (Acts 10:38).

Steve Young

Introduction

Mother Teresa reportedly kept the following statement hanging on her wall:

> *People are often unreasonable, illogical,*
> *   and self-centered;*
> *Forgive them anyway.*
>
> *If you are kind, people may accuse you of*
> *   selfish, ulterior motives;*
> *Be kind anyway.*
>
> *If you are successful, you will win some*
> *   false friends and some true enemies;*
> *Succeed anyway.*
>
> *If you are honest and frank, people may*
> *   cheat you;*
> *Be honest and frank anyway.*
>
> *What you spend years building, someone*
> *   could destroy overnight;*
> *Build anyway.*

*If you find serenity and happiness,
  they may be jealous;
Be happy anyway.*

*The good you do today, people will
  forget tomorrow;
Do good anyway.*

*Give the world the best you have,
  and it may never be enough;
Give the world the best you've got anyway.*

*You see, in the final analysis,
  it is between you and God;
It never was between you and them anyway.*

We live in a day when many are afraid to speak their feelings about sacred beliefs and values for fear of being mocked or becoming the brunt of merciless jokes. Standing up for goodness, righteousness, virtue, chastity, honesty, dignity, and self-control has become old-fashioned and out-dated. Defending traditional morality has even been labeled intolerant, prudish, and self-righteous. Words such as truth, morals, and values have become shrouded in intellectual jargon by scholars and cynics who have labeled their use as preachy or overbearing. But as Mother Teresa believed, "in the final analysis, it is between you and God" not between you and what others think.

Many people are so afraid of offending special interest groups, of being made fun of, or of suffering criticism for defending what's right that they have become lukewarm about what it means to be good. They have lost their desire for standing up and speaking out. As a result, families, communities, cities, and nations are falling apart.

The handbook of successful living for centuries—the

Bible—lies unread in many homes, gathering dust and being replaced by the literature of pop culture. Thus many people are unaware of the warnings of the Old Testament prophet Isaiah. Writing of our day, he said, "Woe unto them that call evil good, and good evil; that put darkness for light, and light for darkness; that put bitter for sweet, and sweet for bitter! Woe unto them that are wise in their own eyes, and prudent in their own sight! . . . Which justify the wicked for reward, and take away the righteousness of the righteous from him!" (Isaiah 5:20–21, 23).

Is that not happening today in all segments of our society? If ever there were a time to stand for what is right and let our light shine, it is now! Writing to the people of Thessalonica, the apostle Paul declared, "Ye are all the children of light, and the children of the day: we are not of the night, nor of darkness" (1 Thessalonians 5:5). To the residents of Rome, Paul admonished, "The night is far spent, the day is at hand: let us therefore cast off the works of darkness, and let us put on the armour of light" (Romans 13:12).

The day of standing up and being counted has arrived. It is a time to "cast off the works of darkness" and "put on the armour of light." Being good means to live the basic Judeo-Christian values and standards that have provided so much guidance and happiness throughout the ages. It is to live the Golden Rule. It is to lift and love, to serve and shine. It is to do as Mother Teresa did. No matter what others thought or said, she forgave anyway. She was kind anyway. She succeeded anyway. She was honest and frank anyway. She built anyway. She was happy anyway. She did good anyway. She gave the world the best she had anyway.

I once saw a picture of her gnarled, chapped, disfigured,

wrinkled, worn hands and feet. They reflected her life story. She followed Christ. She loved. She was good.

Would not the world be a better place if more of us did our best to be good? Would there not be more love, hope, faith, and charity? Would there not be less suffering, abuse, and hatred? Being good certainly would have made a difference to the inhabitants of the ancient cities of Sodom and Gomorrah. Abraham, however, could not find even ten good people willing to shine above the darkness that surrounded them.

We may not be able to change *the* world, but we can change *our* world. As J. R. R. Tolkien reminded us in his epic fantasy, *The Lord of the Rings*, "It is not our part to master all the tides of the world, but to do what is in us for the succour of those years wherein we are set, uprooting the evil in the fields that we know, so that those who live after may have clean earth to till. What weather they shall have is not ours to rule" (*The Return of the King* [New York: Ballantine, 1983], 171).

Why are so many of us often afraid to stand up for what we believe to be right? Why do we fear what others may think of us? Marianne Williamson answered those questions when she wrote:

"Our deepest fear is not that we are inadequate. Our deepest fear is that we are powerful beyond measure. It is our light, not our darkness, that most frightens us. We ask ourselves, Who am I to be brilliant, gorgeous, talented, fabulous? Actually, who are you *not* to be? You are a child of God. Your playing small doesn't serve the world. There's nothing enlightened about shrinking so that other people won't feel insecure around you. We are all born to make manifest the glory of God that is within us. It's not just in some of us; it's in everyone. And as we let our own light shine, we unconsciously give other people permission to do the same. As we're liberated from our own fear, our presence automatically liberates others" (*Return to Love* [New York: HarperCollins, 1992], 165).

I hope that this book will help liberate you from your fear to do good so that your goodness may liberate others.

In the following chapters I will discuss the philosophy that there is nothing bad about being good. I will discuss the powers that come to us from being good and that can come in no other way. I will share examples from the lives of good people, past and present, male and female, young and old, who have made a difference in the world by being good to others. I will share stories to fortify and uplift those who are already doing all they can to be good and to help those who have made serious mistakes but who desire to redirect their lives.

I hope you enjoy reading this book as we explore together the benefits of being good and doing good.

Chapter 1

The Worth of a Soul

Christmas Eve 1988 was bitter cold. The thermometer had plunged to zero, and two feet of snow blanketed the ground. It was a day when wise people were inside with the heater turned up, the fire blazing, and a blanket wrapped securely around them.

My family was busily preparing for our customary Christmas Eve activities: opening one gift apiece, eating great food, and participating in the yearly re-enactment of the Christmas story found in the second chapter of Luke in the New Testament. The house was filled with the savory aromas of cooking turkey and freshly baked pumpkin pie—I guess it was, anyway. I couldn't smell a thing. My nose was stuffy, my head pounded, and my entire body ached with the flu. Everyone was having a marvelous time. Everyone but me. Staying in bed, sick, on Christmas Eve was not my idea of fun. However, I knew if I didn't stay down I wouldn't be well enough to enjoy Christmas morning.

I tried to give orders from bed, but no one seemed to pay

much attention, especially when I asked my daughters to let our dog, Grizzly, outside for a few minutes. Deterred by the cold, no one moved until Rebecca, the eldest of my four daughters, finally let Grizzly out the front door. But driven inside by the cold, she didn't stay with him.

A couple hours later I asked if anyone knew where the dog was. Silence greeted my query. Then Rebecca's anxious voice pierced the quiet. "Oh, Dad, I'm sorry!" she exclaimed. "I forgot about the dog!"

I leaped from my bed, dressed quickly, and ran outside, leaving my illness in the bedroom. My case of flu was replaced by the fear of losing my prized golden retriever. When Grizzly failed to respond to my yelling and whistling, I concluded that one of two things had happened: Either he had been stolen or hit by a car. He had always come when called.

My wife, Melanie, and I split up to search for Grizzly through the biting cold. We met a few minutes later at the corner, both frozen and wanting the warmth and comfort of our home. As we were discussing what do to next, a man pulled up in a blue van and asked calmly, "Are you Jack Christianson?"

"Yes, sir. Who are you?"

He told me his name and, with some hesitation, added, "I'm your paperboy's father. Your dog followed my son home from his paper route and was hit by a truck in front of our home. Would you please come and decide what you want to do with the body?"

"Is he dead?" I asked, with little hope in my voice.

"Not yet," he replied sadly. "But I'm not sure how long he'll live."

We climbed into the van in silence and quietly rode to the scene of the accident. Melanie covered her face with her hands, and tears dripped off the back of her hands onto her lap.

Our eyes met, and she communicated a heartfelt message: "I'm sorry, Jack. I know how much you love your dog."

When we arrived at the scene of the accident, a crowd of concerned neighbors stood around the dog's broken body, which was covered with someone's coat. As we approached Grizzly, an animal-control officer arrived with an "ambulance." It was really an animal-control truck with a cage in the back, but I viewed it as an ambulance that would transport Grizzly for treatment.

The sound of my voice brought Grizzly's head up off the cement. His body was stretched across the curb, the front half lying on the sidewalk and the hind legs lying helplessly in the gutter. He tried in vain to get up. Both back legs were shattered. I calmed him by speaking in soft tones and patting him on the head and neck.

I cried as I looked him over. I asked the officer if there was a veterinarian on call somewhere in the vicinity.

"It's Christmas Eve," he said, somewhat hesitantly. "But I'll try anyway."

While he talked with a dispatcher, an older gentleman, bundled up in a winter parka and a dirty baseball cap, approached us slowly.

"That your dog, son?" he asked, trying to fight back tears.

"Yeah."

"There was nothing I could do! He just darted in front of my truck! I didn't even have time to hit the brakes."

"It's okay," I said. "I'm sure there was nothing you could have done."

"I'm sorry, son. I'm sorry."

I felt as bad for him as I did for the dog. He walked away dejected—hands in his pockets and head down, mumbling through tears how sorry he was.

"I found one!" the officer said. "The vet will meet us at his office in fifteen to twenty minutes. He's at the mall finishing his Christmas shopping, but he said your golden retriever was worth stopping everything else."

"Thanks," I muttered as I picked up Grizzly and walked toward the animal-control truck. The man who had brought us to the scene of the accident gave my wife a ride home while the officer and I transported my dog to the veterinarian's office. Melanie arrived at the office shortly after I had carried Grizzly in and placed him on a long, coal-black table. As she watched the doctor and me work on Grizzly, she again tried to hide her tears. Approximately two and one-half hours later the doctor gave me the bad news.

"I'm sorry, Jack. I've done all I can do, short of surgery, and I don't think Grizzly will live through that. It would cost a few hundred dollars, and he'd never make it," he said sadly. "My suggestion is that we put him to sleep. Would you like some time to think about it and to talk it over with your wife?"

"Sure. Thanks," I said, trying to fight back my tears.

Melanie and I decided it would be best to end Grizzly's suffering. So, after a few minutes alone with my faithful friend, I kissed him good-bye, asked him to forgive me, and then asked the doctor to do his part quickly. Within ten seconds after the doctor injected a drug into Grizzly's right front leg, his eyes rolled upward and he was dead. I wept.

Later, while making arrangements for Grizzly's burial, I asked the doctor what he did with the bodies of deceased animals. He said he usually sent them to California. A truck would come for pickup the following Tuesday; the weather was cold enough that Grizzly's carcass would stay frozen until then. I asked what happened when the animals reached California. I was sickened at the response.

"They make fertilizer or glue out of them," the vet said without batting an eye.

I thought about all the glue and white paste I had eaten out of those big white jars in elementary school. My stomach turned at the thought.

I instantly determined that my favorite dog was not going to be used as paste in some elementary school somewhere, ending up on the back side of a picture of Abraham Lincoln or George Washington. I made arrangements to take Grizzly and bury him myself.

When I told the children that our dear friend was gone, they were heartbroken and asked if they could kiss him good-bye. Some people might think it morbid for sweet young girls to kiss a dead, stiff dog, but he was part of our family.

My father arrived later to help with the burial. We put chains on my car tires and drove to the foothills of a large mountain overlooking our little valley. Dad had recently returned home after being out of the country for a little over a year, so we had much to talk about as we fought the frozen ground and rocky soil to dig a grave.

For some strange reason, as I picked away at the earth, thoughts of pioneer mothers leaving their dead children in shallow graves all along the westward trail flashed through my mind. I was only burying a dog. How would I have felt laying a child or spouse to rest under a thin blanket of snow or wrapped in a quilt and placed under a bush? Tears found their way off the end of my nose and to the back of my hand as I tried to hide them from my dad. My feelings ran deep as I felt a new and deeper appreciation for my ancestors. How did they endure?

With these thoughts burning in my mind, we finished our painful task and lifted a large rock in place as a headstone. We rested, leaning on the handles of our shovel and pick. The sun's long white rays filtered through some evening clouds and rested upon us. It was beautiful and peaceful but bitter cold. I broke the silence by asking my dad a question. Our ensuing conversation proved to have a profound influence on my life.

"Can you believe I feel this way over a silly dog?"

"No!" he quickly answered. "You've lost several dogs and other animals, son. Why would this one be so different?"

I don't remember my reply, but my next question began a process of profound thought that led to a rich, religious experience.

"Dad, if you and I as mortals can weep at the loss of a dog, how must God feel when he loses one of his children or sees people suffer?"

"What?" he asked.

"Think about it. If we, as mortals, with all our frailties and imperfections, can weep when we lose a pet, cannot God, the Almighty, the perfect one, weep when his children choose to abandon him or treat each other poorly?"

There on the hillside overlooking the valley where my dad had raised me, we had a deep religious experience discussing the worth of souls and the value of people in the sight of God. It was too cold to talk for long, but seeds were planted deeply within my heart and soul that would not be forgotten with the melting snow. I have been reminded many times since then that every human being is of great worth and value—of far more value to God and to each other than my dog was to me.

I remember when our daughter's hamsters, Josey and Marilyn, died. It was a sad occasion for everyone in our home but me. To me the hamsters were just rodents that ran all night, every night, in a squeaking metal wheel. When I removed the wheel, they decided to climb the water bottle at night and bang it against their glass cage. They drove me crazy! But to our daughter Molly, they were beloved pets. When Josey died, nobody said much. But when Marilyn died, tears trickled down our eight-year-old's face as the cage was cleaned out for the last time and the pet was placed in a shoe box and buried in the backyard.

A similar tragedy occurred when I cleaned the fish tank belonging to another daughter. Two small fish flipped out of my net and slipped down the drain in the bathroom sink. You would have thought I had committed murder! Our daughter Rebecca cried over her fish.

We mortals cry over the loss of animals and physical possessions. Why, then, do we not weep more over each other's suffering? Why are we so intolerant of others? Why are we so cruel? Why when we see others pursuing lifestyles that are self-destructive or destructive of others do we think, *It's their life, and they can destroy it if they want to?* We do all we can to provide our pets with the most comfortable life possible. What about people? Can't we more readily say hello when we pass others on the street? Can't we lift one another rather than put one another down? What kind of world would this be if we cared for people as much as we care for animals?

As children of God, we are more than advanced animals; we are of divine origin. We all have eternal worth and deserve to be treated with dignity. By believing that human beings are of great worth, we can change the world. Jesus taught, "Greater love hath no man than this, that a man lay down his life for his friends" (John 15:13). You and I will probably not be required to lay down our lives for anyone, but we are called upon daily to be kind and considerate and to lift and inspire.

A few days after Grizzly's death I tried to find a puppy to take his place. I contacted the people who had sold us Grizzly, and they offered to give us his mother if we would breed her with a particular male and then give them a puppy. After seeing the mother dog, Ginger, I agreed to their condition. Ginger looked just like Grizzly, but she was two or three inches shorter, and her neck and head were not as large. I brought her home and provided a place for her in the garage.

A few months later my daughters helped me deliver nine golden retriever puppies. As the puppies were born, I couldn't help but ask the question: "Girls, if you and I can get so excited over the birth of puppies, can we not get excited when people find happiness and fulfillment in their lives?" They thought my question was an odd way to teach a lesson, but I gave them something to think about.

The world is full of wonderful, good people. Many are doing the best they can with what they have been given. If we all do the best we can with what we have, things almost always work out for our good over time.

What's wrong with trying to make the world a better place? What's wrong with helping people be happy as they venture through their circle of life? What's so bad about being good and doing unto others as we would have them do unto us, caring for others and their happiness, and finding and living by true and correct principles that apply to all humans regardless of race, religion, or nationality?

In the classic movie *Fiddler on the Roof,* Tevye feels that a poor tailor is not wealthy enough to marry his daughter, so in frustration the tailor cries out, "Even a poor tailor is entitled to some happiness!" I agree. Everyone on earth is entitled not to just some happiness but a great amount of happiness. Happiness, however, often depends on making correct decisions. Every decision is accompanied by a consequence. If we want to be happy, we must learn to make right decisions based on correct principles.

Chapter 2

What's So Bad about Being Good?

If you're like most Americans, you have seen the classic film *The Wizard of Oz* many times. As a young boy, I could hardly wait to watch it during each annual showing on TV. This was long before videos could be rented on every street corner. As I grew older and was playing football in college, I still enjoyed watching it. Some of my fellow players would join me but would never own up to it around their teammates.

I have lost count of how many times I have watched *The Wizard of Oz*. When videocassette recorders became popular, my wife and I won one in a drawing at a local video store. Shortly thereafter *The Wizard of Oz* was on television, and somehow we figured out how to use the machine to record the movie.

For about a year, *The Wizard of Oz* was the only video we owned. We had three young daughters at the time. Guess what they wanted to watch almost every day? Sometimes on weekends and holidays they would watch it two or three times a day. I grew to appreciate it in a way I would never have thought possible. Many words from the movie have become bywords in our home. For about a year, one of our daughters pretended that her name was Dorothy; she even named a stuffed animal "Toto too!"

The phrase "Toto too" comes from a scene in which Dorothy is preparing to fly home to Kansas with the wizard in his hot-air balloon. As Toto darts after a cat, the Wizard loses control of the balloon and leaves without Dorothy. Glinda (the good witch) floats onto the scene in a large clear bubble. She tells Dorothy she has always had the power to go home but that in order to do so she had to learn something very important: No matter where she goes in the world, there is no place like home. With this knowledge, Glinda says, Dorothy can use the ruby slippers to return home. Before clicking her heels together three times, Dorothy asks, "Toto too?" Glinda responds, "Toto too."

After watching *The Wizard of Oz* a couple hundred times, I grew to love it more and more. I learned many lessons from its symbolism. For example, the first few minutes are filmed in black and white, as are the last five minutes. The movie doesn't use full color until Dorothy goes "over the rainbow"—leaving behind the sheltered environment of Kansas and seeing the world from a new perspective.

Dorothy and the movie's other memorable characters teach interesting lessons. Dorothy is a symbol of a sweet, innocent girl from "Your Town, USA," who enters a world where the wicked try to capture her and steal her power source, the ruby slippers. The other characters in Dorothy's company suggest an underlying theme of the movie: You are what you think you are.

For instance, the Scarecrow believes he has no brain

because he has been told that there is nothing in his head but straw. However, he thinks up every plan during the entire adventure. The Scarecrow has always had a brain but has believed people who have told him otherwise. Later, when the Wizard gives him the degree of "Doctor of Thinkology," the Scarecrow instantly raises his finger to his wise head and quotes a mathematical equation. He simply needed someone to tell him he had a brain. He then believed it himself.

The Tin Man supposedly has no heart, yet he is always being told not to cry or he will rust. The Wizard later hangs a mechanical heart around his neck, and when Dorothy says her final good-byes to her friends, the Tin Man tells her, "Now I know I've got a heart because it's breaking." He had always had a heart. He just needed someone to tell him that the love others had for him was proof of his own loving heart.

The Cowardly Lion—my favorite character—supposedly has no courage, but once he joins the group, he often leads the way. When he first encounters Dorothy, the Tin Man, the Scarecrow, and Toto, he puts on a display of courage and tries to capture and bite Toto. But his sense of cowardice is confirmed when, after being slapped on the nose by Dorothy, he cries and carries on, lamenting his lack of courage. He later receives a medal in recognition of the courage he displayed while helping to rescue Dorothy. As the Wizard pins the medal to his mane, the no-longer Cowardly Lion exclaims, "Ain't it the truth!" Again, once someone believed in him, he believed in himself.

The movie's greatest scene and lesson, however, occur earlier. Dorothy and Toto have been captured by the Wicked Witch, who has locked them up in a room high in her castle. As a draining hourglass forebodes Dorothy's

doom, her friends break open the room's large wooden
doors. After exchanging quick hugs, they run down the
stairs to the castle's main court. Suddenly, their escape is
cut off when huge double doors slam shut before them.
They hear an evil cackle from the Wicked Witch, standing
on a balcony above them. "Going so soon?" she asks. "I
wouldn't hear of it. Why, my little party's just beginning."
Several guards then appear and surround Dorothy and her
friends.

As the Wicked Witch laughs in delight, enjoying her
apparent victory, the Scarecrow quickly thinks of a plan.
He sees a rope leading to a chandelier hanging directly
above the guards. He grabs the ax from the Tin Man and
cuts the rope. The chandelier falls on the guards, creating a
diversion that allows Dorothy and her friends to run to the
top of the wall surrounding the castle. But each way they
try to run, guards cut them off. They are soon surrounded
in a small tower room lighted by burning torches. A bucket
of water, fortunately, sits within Dorothy's reach.

"Well, ring-around-a-rosy, a pocketful of spears!" cackles
the Wicked Witch as she enters the tower room. "Thought
you'd be pretty foxy, did you? Well, the last to go will see
the first three go before her and her mangy little dog too!"

She then stretches her broom toward one of the torches.
The broom catches fire—symbolic of evil, death, and
destruction—and she lights the Scarecrow's arm, taunting,
"How about a little fire, Scarecrow?"

Dorothy immediately reaches for the bucket of water—
symbolic of purity, cleanliness, and life. In horror, the
witch screams, "Don't touch that water!" Splash! The
water covers the witch's face, hands, and torso. As she
begins to melt, she whines, "Oh, what a world, what a

world! Who would have thought a good little girl like you could destroy my beautiful wickedness!"

As smoke rises from the black heap of the Wicked Witch's clothing, a guard declares, "Hail to Dorothy! The Wicked Witch is dead!" One good little girl had destroyed all the "beautiful wickedness" in an entire land.

Oh, what a world, what a world we live in today—full of wickedness and corruption. But like Dorothy in the land of Oz, good men and women and good boys and girls can make this world a better place. If we live according to true, correct, and time-tested principles, we really can make a difference and help destroy some of the "beautiful wicked-ness" that surrounds us.

Often as I travel and speak to various adult and youth groups, I hear some interesting arguments about being *too* good. Many say, "It's okay to be good, but don't be too good or people will think you're weird or a geek or a goody-goody."

Great men and women throughout history would have ignored such arguments. Many, like Christ, Abraham Lincoln, and Joan of Arc, lost their lives because of their goodness. What about all the unknowns who lived quiet lives of service, blessed countless others, and died without fortune and fame? What about the millions who have given their lives to preserve freedom for others they never knew or met? Why did they make the ultimate sacrifice?

The early 1940s brought much sorrow to the small town where my mother and father were reared. In many ways this town was not much different than most rural American towns during the early 1940s, but the area suffered an unusually high death rate for servicemen during World War II. In this town, few lives were untouched, and almost everyone in town lost a family member or friend to the cause of freedom. My family was no exception.

To this day my father feels deeply the loss of his cousin Allen "Big Chris" Christianson. "Big Chris" was flying in a P-38 in North Africa when his plane collided with a B-17 bomber while landing. Chris did not survive the crash. Each Memorial Day, I walk with my dad to Chris's grave and place flowers near his headstone. I hear the same story and see the same sorrow in my father's eyes as he recounts what happened and as he remembers the good times he and Chris had before the war separated them.

Each year as we drive into the cemetery, we gaze at the many white crosses positioned in dozens of straight rows. Each cross honors a man or woman from that town who gave his or her life for freedom or who served in the armed forces and died later of other causes.

Positioned in those rows are two crosses that have special significance to my mother's family. Those crosses bear the names of my mother's two older brothers, Franklin and Ralph. Both saw action in the South Pacific. Franklin was killed aboard the USS *Walk,* a naval destroyer, and Ralph served on the USS *Talledega.* Ralph did not die until the 1970s, but the two brothers' lives were much entwined in January 1945. Franklin was serving as an officer, Ralph as a signalman. Both of their ships were engaged in the battle of Lingayen Gulf in the Philippines.

The *Talledega* was a troopship trying to land troops on a beach, and the *Walk* was a destroyer in a fleet of American ships providing protection for the troops so they could successfully take the beach and fulfill their mission. The casualty rate of those landing on the beach from the troopships was extremely high. All aboard knew that chances of survival were slim to none, but they bravely attempted to fulfill their missions to provide freedom for future generations. On a typical beach landing, the casualty rate could be as high as 85 percent for the first wave of soldiers and marines and 50 percent for the second wave. It is difficult to imagine what went through the minds of those valiant men as they contemplated giving their young lives so others might be free. Perhaps the scripture referred to in chapter one filled some of their minds and hearts: "Greater love hath no man than this, that a man lay down his life for his friends" (John 15:13).

For five days, the USS *Walk* did everything it could to protect the *Talledega* and other ships from Japanese air strikes. On the sixth day of the battle, six Japanese suicide bombers attacked. Five were shot down before they reached any ships; the pilot of the sixth, evidently realizing he would never reach the *Talledega* or other troopships, decided instead to blow up the *Walk*. As the pilot flew his plane toward the deck of the *Walk*, Franklin stood on the bridge watching a teenage gunner firing at the oncoming plane. The tracer bullets were missing the oncoming plane badly. Franklin knew that if the plane released its bomb and hit the ship, his entire crew could be killed and the troopships placed in jeopardy.

In an instant, Franklin did his duty as an officer. He ran from the bridge to the antiaircraft gun, threw the young sailor down some stairs to safety, and began firing at the suicide bomber. The pilot was shot and killed before he could release his bomb, but Franklin could not stop the plane from hitting the ship. He kept firing to the very end. The plane hit the ship right where Franklin was standing, killing him instantly. The ship survived because the bomb on the plane did not explode. The young gunner survived because he was thrown to safety. Ralph and the *Talledega* survived because the suicide planes never reached their decks. Franklin lost his life preserving the lives of others. He died a hero—a true war hero. He was buried at sea, and none of his family or friends ever saw his remains. His beautiful wife, daughter, and unborn son were left without their husband and father so others might be free. He laid down his life for his friends, his brother, and for you and me.

Each time I enter the cemetery in my parents' hometown, these events come to mind. I can't share all that happened and how the lives of the teenage gunner and my Uncle Ralph turned out, but their lives were forever altered that January day in 1945. My life and the lives of my grandparents, mother, uncles, and aunt were altered as well.

Are we living good, honest, moral lives that show gratitude for all the Franklins who have willingly given their lives for our freedom? Or do we give little thought to the sacrifice of others? Most people who have lived or ever will live on the earth will never hear of my Uncle Franklin, but his good life has influenced many in many ways. Alexis de Tocqueville once said, "America is great because America is good. If America ceases to be good, America will cease to be great!"

Some argue that if you're too good, you are hypocritical or have a holier-than-thou attitude. I don't agree. Being good, as I define it, leads to the opposite of a holier-than-thou attitude. A truly good person respects others as individuals of great and infinite worth; thus my fellow human beings are at least my equal and perhaps even my superior in some ways.

We may encounter plenty of hypocrites and self-righteous people in our dealings with others, but why should that hinder us from being all we should be? We can't spend our time and energy worrying about things over which we have no control. We can't walk around waiting for someone to disagree with us or to offend us. I can't anyway. I haven't got time or energy to let hypocrites hurt my feelings.

Some people don't live what they teach. They suffer from the same problem you and I do: They're mortals! They make mistakes! It will always be thus. Our goal is to do the best we can with what we have and to try to help others do the same. We must lift and inspire, not spend our lives trying to find fault with others.

Let us allow God to take care of those who claim to be better than others, and let us take care of ourselves, remembering and striving to live according to our values and principles. Remembering my name and my family has helped me. I was given my father's name, and I don't want to do anything that would bring shame to that name. Whenever I hear my name, I am reminded of what is expected of me and what kind of man I should be while living and working in a world of imperfect mortals. I am reminded of the teachings of my youth and childhood. I am reminded of my desires to honor and respect my name and what my family represents. I am reminded to be good!

Have you ever been sitting at a funeral and heard people say things about the deceased that you knew were not true? Most of us have on one occasion or another. It's uncomfortable, isn't it? You look at others and smile, wondering if you're at the right funeral. If you're like me, don't you wonder what people will say at your funeral? Will anybody even attend? Will people speak the truth, or will they have difficulty finding anything good to say?

A good friend of my wife didn't have to wonder what

people would say at her funeral. Her life hadn't turned out the way she had hoped, but she had tried to do everything right according to her beliefs. She had married her prince charming, had a family, served her church and community, taught elementary school—everything she could to help things turn out the way she had dreamed as a young girl. Then her husband left her, abandoning her to raise her family alone. If that were not enough, she was diagnosed with a terminal case of cancer. Nevertheless, she never quit believing that she should be good. She did the best she could with what she had. She wrote the following just prior to her death. It inspires me when people scoff at the idea of being good:

"I don't want to drive up to the Pearly Gates in a shiny sports car, wearing beautifully tailored clothes, with my hair expertly coiffed, and with long, perfectly manicured nails. I want to drive up to the Pearly Gates in a station wagon that has Boy Scout equipment in the back seat. I want there to be grass stains on my shoes from mowing Mrs. Schneck's lawn. I want there to be a smudge of peanut butter on my shirt from making sandwiches for a sick neighbor's children. I want there to be a little dirt under my fingernails from helping 4-H'ers plant a garden. I want there to be children's sticky kisses on my cheeks and the tears of a friend on my shoulder. I want God to know that I was really here and that I really lived."

What an attitude! When you die, will God know that you were really here and that you really lived? Will there be dirt under your fingernails or grass stains on your shoes? Will there be sticky kisses on your cheeks or tears of a friend on your shoulder? Or will there be no proof that you were here because, thinking only of yourself, you did so little good that no one else's life was affected? I hope volumes of good will be written about you, proving that you really were here and that you really did live. Be assured that one good boy or girl and one good man or woman *can* make a difference in this world.

Chapter 3

"My Life Is My Message"

Many good individuals have had a great influence on the world. Undoubtedly, each of us has a personal hero or heroine who has motivated us to do our best and to be our best. Heroes do not exist only in the pages of books or on TV and movie screens.

Perhaps you and I may never be great in the eyes of the world or influence great multitudes of people. Perhaps our names will never be etched in the pages of history. Our words may never be quoted. We may never write a bestseller or be a movie star or sports idol. We may never become the president or CEO of a corporation. But what if we quietly live our lives doing the best we can? What if we are just good, committed moms and dads, sons and daughters, brothers and sisters? What if we are good neighbors and loyal friends? What if we are just simple, down-to-earth people with our heads on straight and our priorities in order?

What would happen to our homes, our communities, our nation, and our world if we were patient, honest, and kind? What would transpire if we became honest bankers, car salespeople, construction workers, teachers, actors, businesspeople, musicians, lawyers, and so on? What would happen to many of our social problems and challenges if we started caring more about each other?

You may think I live in a dream world to believe that most people could ever live in the way described above. But think about how this world would change if more of us really cared about being good. I believe in the adage "One is often a multitude," and I love this statement by Gandhi: "My life is my message." If we truly believe that being good makes a difference and that fame and fortune are not prerequisites to influencing people, we will let our lives be our message.

Each Christmas many of us enjoy watching the classic film *It's a Wonderful Life,* starring Jimmy Stewart as George Bailey and Donna Reed as his faithful wife. George feels his life has been a failure because he never pursued his dream to become an architect and travel the world. He simply lived out his life in the same little town where he was born, and there he helped friends and loved ones fulfill their dreams.

After losing money he needed to maintain his savings and loan business, George feels his life has been a waste. He decides to end it all by jumping off a bridge into a river, but he is saved by an angel named Clarence, who tries to persuade George that he really has had a wonderful life. Clarence shows George a vision of what would have happened if he had never lived. In the vision, George's brother never grew up to be a war hero because George was not there to save him from drowning at age four. George's wife never married but lived alone and unhappy, and their children were never born because George wasn't there. The local pharmacist went to prison and then became a drunk because George wasn't there to correct the pharmacist's potentially harmful mistake in filling a prescription. Many townspeople never purchased or built homes because George Bailey wasn't there to loan them money through the savings and loan association. George recognizes that he has enjoyed "a wonderful life." His little good deeds had affected the lives of many other people.

Like George, many of us may feel that our lives are not very important to the entire scheme of things in the universe. The next time you begin to feel that you make little difference, consider all those whose lives would be different if you did not exist. Some of you may feel that others would be better off without you, but before you fall into that trap, remember George Bailey. He had no way of knowing he was influencing so many. You don't either! You must not lose hope. You must not give up. You do make a difference. You just need a Clarence in your life to help you see more clearly.

Your life has a profound impact on many others. None of us knows the future or how our lives today will influence future generations. But being good and doing good can make a profound difference.

If you have slipped and wonder if there is a way to find peace and happiness, keep trying. You can make it. A happy life is worth every effort and pain. If you have lost hope, it is not too late. Do whatever it takes to change your life, and do it now. If changing means getting on your knees and asking for help, do it. If it means asking someone for forgiveness or help, do it. Don't wait for everything to be perfect before you start.

If you need to get into a treatment program or begin taking medication, start today. Don't wait until you hit rock bottom. Begin doing whatever it takes to be good. Eat your pride if necessary.

The greatest contribution any of us can make toward personal, community, family, or world peace is to live a good, clean life and help those who will listen to do the same. Happiness is inseparably connected with decent, clean behavior, and behavior is greatly improved when linked to traditional standards and values. Values applied to everyday life produce positive results in individuals, families, communities, and nations.

At the beginning of this chapter I mentioned that most of us have a hero or heroine who has motivated us to be better. Many heroes, both ancient and modern, fill my personal hall of fame. Most of those who have deeply influenced my life can be read about in the pages of history and scripture. Some that I mention here, however, are likely to be unknown to you, yet they had a profound impact on the world in which they lived. With their goodness, they destroyed a lot of wickedness. Each was or is just one good boy, girl, man, or woman. Perhaps they can give you hope and encouragement and influence your life in some small degree.

1. The first person on my list remains unknown to me by name. I observed her some years ago when my wife and I took our children to a Special Olympics track meet. We wanted them to gain an appreciation of and love for those less fortunate than themselves. We knew that Special Olympians were people with great spirits and treasures on the inside who happen to have mental or physical disabilities. Despite their outward appearances or abilities, they are real people with real feelings and needs. Though none of these athletes will ever be famous or go down as

champions in the record books of the world, they are all champions nonetheless because they do their very best.

We wanted to teach our children this vital lesson about life. We wanted them to know that the motto of the Special Olympics is not just for Special Olympians but is a tremendous motto for success in life: "Let me win. But if I cannot win, let me be brave in the attempt." We hoped our children would gain faith and bravery to face anything life has to offer.

The track meet proved to be the teacher we had hoped it would be. Our children loved it once they got used to the open show of affection and the athletes' mannerisms. They watched the "huggers" hug every participant after each event. They felt the love and warmth of athletes and volunteers. The most significant lesson came with the women's 100-meter dash.

One of the participants was a woman in her twenties with Down's syndrome. She appeared to be as wide as she was tall. She had split her pants, and a large safety pin had been fastened in a futile attempt to keep her pants up.

When the starting gun fired, the runners took off. The woman immediately fell behind the other runners. She had difficulty putting one leg in front of the other, but she persisted nevertheless. Then it happened. The safety pin popped, the pants fell to her ankles, and she fell flat on her face.

I wanted to jump from the stands and help her. Before I could move, however, she stood, pulled up her pants, held them together in front with one hand, and hobbled to the end of the track. When she crossed the finish line she fell into the outstretched arms of a hugger. Everyone cheered for her as if she had won the race. Tears welled up in my eyes as I witnessed her courage. I knew that if this had happened to me I would have found a place to hide rather than finish the race.

That is not the end of the story, however. When the medals were awarded, she stood on the platform, still holding her pants together with one hand. When presented with her medal, she bent over so it could be placed around her neck. As she straightened up, she was overcome by the excitement of receiving a medal. She raised both hands above her head in triumph and waved excitedly to the crowd, forgetting about her pants. They fell to her ankles again. She didn't seem to mind that she stood before a large crowd in her underwear. She had done her best and been brave in the attempt.

I hope my family never forgets the feelings generated that day. We had watched a true champion, one who did her best. We had been taught by a mentally and physically challenged woman who had no idea she was teaching us. The life she lived was her message to others; she didn't have to speak. She wasn't trying to teach or influence for good, she just did! That day I learned to do my best and to not compare myself with anyone else. Doing our best with what we have been given means success.

2. The late Mother Teresa of Calcutta was an inspiration to many. Joyfully, I watched her on news broadcasts. She spent her entire adult life giving to and sharing with others, showing the entire world that one good woman can influence countless millions for good. She didn't do anything to be noticed; she simply cared about relieving human suffering and bringing joy and happiness to the lives of others. She had a special gift for blessing the less fortunate and the downtrodden.

"We must not drift away from the humble works, because these are the works nobody will do," Mother

Teresa wrote. "It is never too small. We are so small we look at things in a small way. But God, being almighty, sees everything great. Therefore, even if you write a letter for a blind man or you just sit and listen, or you take the mail for him, or you visit somebody or bring a flower to somebody—small things—or wash clothes for somebody, or clean the house. Very humble work, that is where you and I must be. For there are many people who can do big things. But there are very few people who will do the small things" (*Love: A Fruit Always in Season,* ed. Dorothy S. Hunt [San Francisco: Ignatius Press, 1986], 26).

I once read about Mother Teresa sheltering a dying derelict whose body was crawling with worms. She said it took three hours to pick all the worms from his body. The emaciated man murmured gratefully that he had lived like an animal but could now die like an angel. Mother Teresa related how he went home to God with a joyful heart because he had received tender love and care.

Even if Mother Teresa hadn't affected millions for the better, she had made a difference in the life of one worm-ridden man. Would you have had the stomach and the patience to sit for three hours and remove worms from a derelict's dirty, smelly body? Mother Teresa showed that every person has value. No job is too small when it comes to helping people have dignity and relieving human suffering.

3. Another of my heroes is a student who had a profound impact on me and on many others who knew him. He was somewhat disruptive in class at times yet so fun to be around that it was difficult to get after him. He liked to call me by my first name just to see if he could get a rise out of me—a strategy that often worked. At times he drove me crazy.

After his graduation he worked at a local mall. I had no idea he was working there. He saw me coming down the mall corridor one day with my family. He hid behind a rack of clothing until I walked by and then jumped on my back. He started to laugh when he realized he had caught me by complete surprise. I fell to the floor, and he rubbed his knuckles back and forth across my head—a painful trick for someone who is bald on top! He laughed until he was sick, and everyone who watched found the scene quite funny.

That was the last time I saw him alive. Steven Eugene Blake met a tragic death in 1988 while saving the life of a person whom, to my knowledge, he had never met. I keep a copy of his obituary in my speaking notes and look at it nearly every week. It may sound strange to carry a copy of a former student's obituary, but the obituary helps me stay focused on why I do what I do, on what my motives are, and on how valuable each individual is.

Steven was only twenty-one, and his whole life lay before him. Yet one split-second decision to serve another ended his young, promising life. A man was working on an electrical sign when the boom on the truck that held up the sign knocked a high voltage wire down on him. Steven and his friends saw the accident and ran to the scene to assist the man, who was being electrocuted. Steven evidently didn't hesitate to remove the man from the power line, but as he grabbed hold and pulled him away, electricity running through the man's body jolted Steven. He was thrown forward onto the very line from which he had just pulled the worker. Steven was severely burned and died a few days later at a local hospital.

He had given the ultimate sacrifice—his life. Why? To save the life of a stranger, a man in his seventies who had just remarried and who was the father of a young child. It will be a long time before I forget the news broadcast showing the man weeping in gratitude. "Why would a young man with his whole life ahead of him do a thing like this for an old man like me?" he asked, his voice choked with emotion.

I knew Steven well, not only as one of his teachers at school but also as his neighbor. He wasn't perfect, and I'm not trying to paint him bigger than life. But he lived what he believed, and he knew that giving his life for a "friend" is the greatest form of love.

Is that why you and I serve or want to be good? Do we do it for love, without concern about whether we are recognized or paid for our efforts?

At the graveside service, I watched pallbearers cry as they placed Steven's casket on green straps stretched over the grave. I watched his family agonize over the loss of a beautiful son and brother. One of the pallbearers approached me, put his arms around me, and said, "Isn't it tragic that something like this has to happen to make us realize what is really important in life?"

I've never forgotten that comment. It is tragic that we must be shaken by death and heartache to keep us focused on the truly important things. Steven Blake's obituary constantly reminds me to do things for love.

4. Stillman Pond was an early nineteenth-century pioneer who brought his family west from Hubbardston, Massachusetts. In September 1846 Stillman and his family became part of the great western migration. The early winter that year brought disease and death. The family was stricken with malaria, cholera, and consumption (tuberculosis).

All the children had malaria when Stillman's wife,

Maria, contracted malaria and consumption. Three of the children soon died and were buried on the plains. Maria's condition rapidly worsened to the point that she could no longer walk. Though weak and sick, she gave birth to twins, who died within a few days. The remaining members of the Stillman Pond family spent the winter in Nebraska living in a tent. Like many other families in the same situation, they suffered much.

Journal accounts verify the following regarding four other children who perished: "On Wednesday the 2nd of December 1846, Laura Jane Pond, age 14 years, . . . died of chills and fever." On "Friday, the 4th of December 1846, Harriet M. Pond, age 11 years, . . . died with chills." Three days later, on "Monday, the 7th of December, 1846, Abigail A. Pond, age 18 years, . . . died with chills." Five weeks later, on "Friday, the 15th of January, 1847, Lyman Pond, age 6 years, . . . died with chills and fever." A few months later Stillman Pond's wife also died (James E. Faust, "The Refiner's Fire," *Ensign,* May 1979, 54).

Crossing the plains, Stillman Pond lost nine children and a wife, but he became an outstanding colonizer and a great leader in the West. He did not lose his faith or his desire to live and do good. He did not quit but went forward and made the best of a horribly tragic situation.

5. In his book *The Moral Compass,* William J. Bennett retells the ancient, moving story of the wives of Weinsberg. These women deeply influenced their world with fidelity and goodness. Unbeknownst to them, their act of selfless service to their husbands influenced many future generations. But they were not thinking of all the people they would bless by being good; they just wanted to help those whom they loved.

The story took place in Germany in 1141. Wolf, the

duke of Bavaria, was trapped inside his castle at Weinsberg. Outside the castle, the army of Frederick, the duke of Swabia, and his brother, the emperor Konrad, waited to destroy Wolf. The siege had been long, and Wolf knew his surrender was imminent. As messengers rode back and forth with proposed terms, Wolf and his officers sadly prepared to give up to their hated enemy.

However, the wives of Weinsberg were not ready to give up all they held dear. They sent a message to Konrad, asking the emperor to allow all the women safe passage out of the castle with as many of their valuables as they could carry. Konrad granted their request. When the castle gates were opened, the women came out carrying their most valuable possessions. The armies of Konrad and Frederick were stunned. The women did not carry gold or jewels. Rather, "each one was bending under the weight of her husband, whom she hoped to save from the vengeance of the victorious host."

Evidently Konrad's heart was touched. The story records that he was brought to tears by the extraordinary performance. With a generous and merciful nature, he assured the women of their husbands' safety and freedom. The duke of Bavaria, his men, and their wives were all invited to a banquet, and peace was negotiated on much more favorable terms than expected (*The Moral Compass: Stories for a Life's Journey* [New York: Simon & Schuster, 1995], 519).

Afterward the castle mount became known as the Hill of *Weibertreue,* or "woman's fidelity." I include these women on my list of heroes and heroines because they understood the value of family and personal relationships. Seasoned warriors and bitter enemies melted with their example of goodness, fidelity, and loyalty.

I marvel at the great influence for good many of my schoolteachers and religious leaders have had and continue to have on my life. Their simple yet great examples of patience, love, and determination have helped me strive to teach as they have taught. I wonder why some of these teachers did not give up on me; perhaps they could see something I could not.

When I enter a classroom today, I understand. As I look into the sea of student faces, some appear to have my young face. I think back and then try harder not to give up on those who fight so defiantly not to be taught. Perhaps each of them will someday influence for good many others, helping them to see that this truly is a wonderful life.

Chapter 4

The Interruption

During my first year of teaching, I walked into a fellow teacher's office one afternoon. On the wall was a sign that read, "You are not the interruption of my life but the purpose for it." The sign did not make sense to me for quite some time. Now, after years of teaching high school and college students, the sign has become my mission statement. It has greatly influenced my attitude toward those who frequently come to my office with so many needs. They are young and inexperienced, and they want to know much. They have many questions about life, including what to study, how to make money, and whom to date and marry.

In their inexperience, many students seem to think that teachers don't have anything to do or prepare if they are in their offices or are not teaching a class. Some even ask, "Why do you need to prepare? You've taught long enough that it just happens, doesn't it?" I wish! To stay fresh and current, teachers must prepare daily, and to avoid burnout, teachers must work at "keeping the saw sharp." However, so many interruptions occur that often it is almost impossible to complete needed preparation, writing, and paperwork without taking work home, working weekends, or staying after hours. It is easy to tire of continually meeting with students and rarely having time for my "real work."

Teaching is similar to other occupations in that if teachers spend all their time "sawing," they soon become dull and ineffective in their work. Without renewal and sharpening, teachers can easily become cynical or negative like the longtime teacher who told me my first year that I had made a mistake in becoming a teacher. He said it is naïve to believe that anyone can really make a difference in someone's life by teaching. He told me to "get real" and not to have high expectations. "Students don't want to learn, and it is a waste of time to try to teach them anything," he said.

One day when I was feeling extremely pressured, I had an experience that taught me the meaning of the phrase I had observed years earlier: "You are not the interruption of my life but the purpose for it." I had experienced the lesson of the phrase many times, but this time it entered my mind and heart with power, changing me!

I had left my office for a drink of water and a quick trip to the rest room. When I exited the rest room, I noticed a somewhat dejected-looking student who was approximately seven months pregnant. Evidently, she was waiting for one of my colleagues.

She asked if I knew where he was and when he would return. I told her he would be out of town for two weeks. She looked heartsick and started to walk away in quiet misery. I proceeded down the hallway to my office.

I thought about asking her if I could help, but immediately I reminded myself that I had a desk full of "work." Besides, I thought, if I could complete my work, I would have time to break away that afternoon and get in nine holes of golf with another student. Then, before I could stop myself, I called down the hall for her to wait. It was obvious that she was in great emotional pain and needed to talk. I asked if I could help even though I was not the trained therapist my colleague was. I inwardly hoped she would say no so I could get back to work.

"Are you sure you have time?" she asked. "I don't want to interrupt."

"I have a few minutes," I responded. "Please come into my office."

I listened for the next hour, nervously fidgeting as I worried about the "work" sitting on my desk. The girl was single. She had just returned from seeing her doctor, who told her that the baby within her suffered from a rare genetic disorder and would not live more than a few hours after birth, if it lived at all. While listening to her story, the words of the sign came into my mind: "You are not the interruption of my life but the purpose for it." As I contemplated the saying, a thought came quietly and peacefully: *This young woman sitting in front of you is your work! This is why you are here! This is why you teach! She, not the papers—as important and necessary as they may be—is your work. This is what teachers should do. Teaching is about people. It's about living, learning, happiness, joy, fulfillment, and peace.*

As she finished sharing her story, she shed tears of gratitude and hope. By having someone to talk to, she could face another day and move ahead.

Who are those who intrude on your "work"? Do you take time to listen to them with your heart rather than just with your ears? Do your most significant others feel like interruptions, or do they know they are the purpose for which you live?

As parents we sometimes forget the importance of nurturing our children spiritually and emotionally as well as mentally and physically. Nurturing requires that we take time to listen and understand our children, remembering what it was like to be a child or an adolescent. As my wife so often reminds me, "Sometimes you act like you were born at age forty-six." It is easy to look upon the needs of our children and others as interruptions rather than as our most sacred responsibilities. As I once heard a wise man say, "Love is not spelled L-O-V-E, it is spelled T-I-M-E." What a simple but profound insight. Our children need our time. If we view them as interruptions, they may come to view family and home as interruptions rather than the major purpose for their lives.

Is it asking too much to spend as much time planning for family activities and family success as we do planning an important work meeting, next summer's garden, or what kind of food we'll serve at our Super Bowl party?

How much of a major schedule adjustment would it take to spend just one evening a week with our families? Would it hurt any of us to arrange our schedules to eat at least a few meals together each week? The tradition of families sitting around the dinner table eating, laughing, sharing experiences, and reading together without interruptions seems to be dying. Sounds old-fashioned, doesn't it? But shouldn't one of the most important pieces of furniture in any home be the dinner table? Shouldn't the most important room in any house be the family room? The size of the family room or dinner table matters little. What matters is that we are together creating memories so that all family members can say with Dorothy, "There's no place like home."

With a feeling of belonging comes an increase in self-esteem and an opportunity to teach and pass on family values and traditions that create stability in the future. Parents and children who love each other will not look upon family time as an interruption but as a source of nourishment and strength to better succeed in a hostile world.

Has supporting children at ball games, concerts, debates, school plays, and other activities become an interruption or a parental purpose? Being a parent takes time, effort, and energy. Parenting is not for wimps or the faint of heart. Because parenting demands that we put off things we would like to accomplish, we may feel that we are wasting our time. Our children, however, don't see our sacrifices that way. They view with love our efforts to support and sustain them.

Charles Francis Adams, the grandson of the second president of the United States, was a successful lawyer, member of the U.S. House of Representatives, and U.S. ambassador to Britain. He was a very busy man, but he kept a diary. On one occasion he wrote of going fishing with his son, recording that he felt he had wasted the day. On the same day, Charles's son, Brooks, wrote in his journal that fishing with his father that day was the most wonderful day of his life.

I know of a young man who, as a senior in high school, sometimes had different feelings than Brooks Adams. He was somewhat embarrassed to have his mom come to his ball games because she was so loud. She would always scream at the top of her lungs, "Come on, Lou! You can do it, Lou! That's my boy!" He was mortified. His dad usually wouldn't sit by her because he too was embarrassed. Instead, he would wander to the sideline or the dugout, or he would go buy popcorn or a drink. She didn't care. She would sit toward the top of the stands so she could stand up. Whenever her boy did anything noteworthy or was about to come to bat, she always let him and everyone else know that he could do whatever needed to be done.

One spring afternoon his feelings changed during an intense baseball game. His team was behind the entire game until tying the score in the seventh inning with four runs. The game went into extra innings, and the other team scored two runs before being put out. Lou's team gathered in the dugout, vowing that they wouldn't lose and that no one would strike out. Lou could talk big because he was the sixth batter up—he didn't think he'd get a chance to make any difference.

The first two batters struck out. The team then somehow managed to score two runs to tie the score again. Lou came to the plate with two outs and one man on base. The moment was something he had dreamed about all his life. He had a chance to be the hero or the goat. It was a true Mark McGwire moment.

As he walked to the plate, butterflies swarmed in the pit of his stomach. His hands were sweating and his heart was pounding. Just then his mother stood up and screamed, "Come on, Lou! You can do it, Lou! You can do it! That's my boy!"

He wanted to hide behind the umpire. Instead, he looked at his mother with a glare that said, "Please love me enough to be quiet." It didn't work. He hoped that his dad would sense his discomfort and just this once get his mom to sit down and quiet down. His dad, however, had found some other errand in the park; he wasn't anywhere near her.

Lou battled the pitcher to a full count—three balls and two strikes. The intensity couldn't have been greater! The battle continued as Lou hit several foul balls. The opposing coach then called time-out and signaled to the bull pen. One of his star relief pitchers trotted to the mound. All he had to do was throw one strike.

During the new pitcher's warm-up, Lou's mother yelled to her son that he didn't need to worry. That was easy for her to say; she didn't have to try to hit a small speeding ball.

The umpire finally signaled the teams to resume play. Lou then raised his hand to signal a time-out, using the break to hit his cleats with his bat. Then, as he dug his right foot into the ground and touched the end of his bat to the corner of the plate, his mom yelled, "Come on, Lou! You can do it, Lou!"

He was so frustrated that he stepped out of the box and again glared at her in disgust. She glared back, clenching her fists and shaking them in his direction. He didn't know what happened at that moment, but his relationship with that dear woman has never been the same since. For the first time in his young eighteen years, he realized that his mother loved him so much that she wasn't afraid of making a fool of herself in front of the entire crowd in order to show him.

He felt the adrenaline pump through his system. He knew he was going to hit that ball. He was going to show his mom that he could do it! And yes, he was her boy and proud of it!

He stepped into the batter's box with a newfound confidence, looking for an inside fastball. The pitcher, however, threw him a slow-breaking curveball. It had his name on it! As it broke, Lou crunched it down the left-field line. It could have been a home run, but it went foul!

Lou decided to swing at the next pitch no matter what—even if the ball was twenty feet high. He'd throw his bat at it if he had to. He was going to hit that ball!

The pitcher wound up and let it rip. It was the same pitch. He couldn't believe it. He waited a split second longer than before, then swung his bat as hard as he could. He still remembers standing at home plate, arms raised in triumph as he watched the ball sail over the left center-field fence. He proudly trotted around the bases, knowing that he was the hero.

What he saw as he crossed home plate astonished him. There in the middle of his ecstatic teammates was his mother. He didn't know how she had jumped the fence and arrived at home plate so quickly, but there she was, jumping up and down and screaming.

After all the hoopla at home plate, she grabbed him and twirled him around, all the time kissing him and whispering, "I knew you could do it, son. I knew you could do it." Then she humbled him to tears. "But son," she said, "I would still love you even if you had struck out." And he knew she did.

His picture was taken for the town newspaper, the crowd soon was gone, and being a hero for a few minutes became a pleasant memory. But his relationship with his mother had changed forever. That afternoon he knew he was not the interruption but rather one of the major purposes for her life.

Chapter 5

Working and Laughing as Families

The Memorial Day holiday is a tender time of year for many people. My family visits two or three cemeteries on that day to honor our dead. One year my wife, her family, and I visited a cemetery where many of my mother-in-law's relatives are buried. Countless flowers of varying colors and arrangements decorated the cemetery lawn. The sun was hot and penetrating. People were everywhere—some clipping grass around headstones, others trying to force flowers to stand upright in small cans or bottles of water. Many people simply stood with solemn faces, reading inscriptions and wandering in their minds to happier days. Their faces revealed memories of times when loved ones still lived, and emptiness and loneliness were yet distant companions. The visit was educational, but it was sad to watch and wonder about the lives of the other visitors.

As we stood by family gravesites, I listened intently as my mother-in-law told stories about each of the individuals whom we had come to honor and remember. Though the sun continued to beat upon us relentlessly, its rays some-how seemed to be reflected and diverted as the stories of our heritage became more important than our physical comfort. We laughed and cried as we talked and listened. It was good to be there.

Before long, the blazing sun took its toll. We loaded up the trunk of the car with empty flower buckets and boxes and made our way to the cemetery gate. We planned to drive to a nearby park and have a picnic. As we carefully tried to avoid people and cars on the narrow one-way cemetery roads, we saw a man, perhaps twenty-five to thirty-five years old, kneeling as he talked to a grave. At first we thought he was injured and calling for help, so we stopped and rolled down the windows to listen. He *was* injured but not physically; rather, he appeared to be emo-tionally devastated. We talked for a moment about whether we should get out of the car and render assistance, but we realized he didn't need us. He needed to let out his pain in solitude.

As we watched, he went from kneeling to lying on the grave. He spread his arms from side to side as if to embrace the buried loved one. This man was beyond grief at the loss of whoever was laid to rest in the grave. His weeping and wailing were more than any of us could bear. Our tears flowed freely, and the lumps in our throats prevented us from speaking. We each felt that we had invaded a sacred moment. We rolled up our windows and slowly drove to the park in silence.

I have learned that most joys are family joys and most sorrows are family sorrows. Our spouses and our families are our primary concerns in this life, and it is okay to weep when loved ones suffer and die. All of us will suffer. All of us will die. We must live together in love so that when

separation comes, whether it be through death or other circumstances, we will be left with few hurtful or embarrassing memories. Life is hard, but amidst all the trials,
heartache, and work there is much to be enjoyed, especially with our loved ones.

You may have heard the saying, "The family that prays
together, stays together." In many cases that is probably
true. But it could also be said, "The family that works
together, laughs together, reads together, stands together,
loves together, and plays together, stays together!" Solid,
stable families take work! If we do not help our children
learn to work, we fail them. I can think of few things more
difficult, yet more rewarding, than working and laughing
beside my children and other family members.

So many families are in crisis today that many wonder
if families are worth all the work, pain, frustration, and
time needed to help them succeed and to help individual
family members be as good as they can be. Whether we
have a traditional family, a single-parent family, or a family
of just one or two members, it's okay to be as good as we
can be. Happiness in any family structure or size is most
likely to be achieved when familial relationships are
founded on faith, prayer, repentance, forgiveness, respect,
love, compassion, charity, humility, mercy, pureness of
heart, work, and wholesome recreational activities. How
can a family, regardless of size or structure, fail if each
member is committed to the Golden Rule: "Whatsoever ye
would that men should do to you, do ye even so to them"?
(Matthew 7:12).

Familial happiness takes work, but work is the business
of life. By helping our children internalize this concept, we
make major strides toward helping them succeed in every

area of their lives. The following passage illustrates this point beautifully:

"There seems to be a superstition among many thousands of our young [men and women] who hold hands and smooch in the drive-ins that marriage is a cottage surrounded by perpetual hollyhocks to which a perpetually young and handsome husband comes home to a perpetually young and ravishing wife. When the hollyhocks wither and boredom and bills appear the divorce courts are jammed. . . .

"Anyone who imagines that bliss is normal is going to waste a lot of time running around shouting that he has been robbed.

"Most putts don't drop. Most beef is tough. Most children grow up to be just people. Most successful marriages require a high degree of mutual toleration. Most jobs are more often dull than otherwise. . . .

"Life is like an old-time rail journey—delays, sidetracks, smoke, dust, cinders and jolts, interspersed only occasionally by beautiful vistas and thrilling bursts of speed.

"The trick is to thank the Lord for letting you have the ride" (Jenkins Lloyd Jones, "Big Rock Candy Mountains," *Deseret News,* 12 June 1973, A4).

Marriage and family life are often a test of mutual tolerance, but we can be happy amidst adversity. One of my wife's friends has observed, "Most of the stress in my life can be traced to one of two sources; I either married it or gave birth to it!"

When we understand and accept life's challenges, we can withstand anything, even the hard lessons. If we have not yet experienced the hard lessons of life, we just need to live a little longer. Each new day has a way of bringing plenty of challenges. The human dramas being acted out in all cultures, races, and economic levels are magnificent teachers.

It has been my privilege for a number of years to teach with a man who goes home several times each day to care for his invalid wife. His love, compassion, and commitment have been a strength to many and have taught me lessons that years of college could not teach. He has become a beacon for his family, students, and fellow teachers. With his permission, I share a personal letter he wrote about his beloved companion of more than thirty-four years:

> My Love,
>
> Still, now over thirty-four years later, I can tell you the exact spot where I first met her, there in the driveway on a warm May afternoon. When I saw her, I thought, *What a beautiful woman.* After a number of dates, one soft summer evening I mustered enough courage to take her in my arms and kiss her for the first time. As I floated on the clouds to my home, I thought I knew all about love, and it was great. Later, as we continued to date, one night when everyone was asleep, I knelt down in front of her chair and asked her to marry me. She asked if I was kidding. I said no. When she said yes, I knew I was in love forever. Months later we were married at an altar. She looked as much like an angel as I hope to see in this life. I willingly said, "I do." We gratefully included God in this special relationship.
>
> One night she anxiously informed me it was time to go to the hospital unless I wanted to be a doctor. Later, I walked into the delivery room and saw her tired but glowing with that precious little life in her arms. I knew that our relationship had changed

forever. I was blessed to witness that divine scene seven more times.

During the years we've been married, many of those years I've been a leader in our church. Sitting on the stand during those years, I've watched this valiant woman with one, two, three, then a whole row of little children, taking care of them all alone. I realize that my love has grown with the lessons of sacrifice and love that I've learned from her.

I've known her to load all of the children in the station wagon and take them twenty miles to shop three different stores just to save a little money. She would then bring everything home, unload it, put it away, fix dinner, and smile lovingly when I would come home and ask what she had done that day.

She has taken a wounded child's head in her hands and administered peace and comfort while others rushed about in a panic. She was so kind and understanding even in times of crisis.

To see her counsel with her children was a revelation. She studied, read, and pondered all she could learn on how to be the best wife and mother possible. Then she went out and applied those principles under the direction of God to the benefit of her little flock. They were bound to her, and she to them.

I watched her happily read to her children, telling them sacred stories, singing them songs. I came to realize her love was pure. Nineteen years ago she was diagnosed with multiple sclerosis. She has waged a courageous battle against the effects of the disease. I've watched her struggle out of bed early in the morning to fix breakfast for her family and tend to their needs.

Now as she sits in her wheelchair and needs me to help her do so many things, I have an important opportunity to serve and support her. I get to do so many services for her. What I enjoy are the personal things that she trusts only me to do.

I see the frustration and fear in her eyes, the need to be assured, comforted, held in my arms. Oh, how much joy I feel to be able to serve this intimate companion of mine. Common, everyday chores become a labor of love for me just as they have been for her all of these years. I still learn about our love in ways I did not anticipate years ago.

Years ago I thought I knew what love was. Now I find that each day brings a new revelation. Love is made from much stronger fabric than I once thought. It is not just the physical attraction that is so glamorized in the popular media of the day. There are so many ways to experience and express the deepening feelings of love that two people feel for each other as they grow together through the marriage covenants that they make with each other and God. I have told my sweetheart, "I am yours, you are mine, and we are God's."

My dear friend is experiencing plenty of struggle and trial without going in search of it. He has taken care of his sweetheart for over twenty years. On that night in May when he fell in love, there was no way of knowing how the final years of their marriage would turn out. Both have become refined and dignified through the fires and crucibles of human experience. They live each day as if it were their last because it may be. They have learned to take advantage of every moment. They know what love is. They have laughed, cried, served, and worked together. In the face of a great trial, they have still been able to raise a happy, successful family.

How are you doing in navigating the stormy waters of life? Are you able to keep your head above water long enough to teach your children how to succeed when life is unfair and difficult? If you feel you are just barely staying afloat, don't quit trying. As you move forward and strive to apply correct principles and values, eventually everything will fall into place or fall out of your life.

I know my parents thought they were not making much headway trying to teach, train, and help me be successful. As you look at your children, realize that things are not always as they seem in your hours of struggle and darkness. Time and patience, unfamiliar words in a fast-paced society, have a way of smoothing out life just as the occasional weeding of a flower bed or garden allows growth and blossoming.

When I was fourteen, my father taught me a very difficult but important lesson about life and work. He taught me to have integrity, to be impeccably honest, and to love people regardless of their circumstances. The lesson came when our community rallied to help hoe six long rows of beets at a local farm. The work had to be finished as soon as possible so that the beets would not be wasted. It was enjoyable work until rain started to fall relentlessly. Everyone ran for cover. After about half an hour, it became evident the rain was not going to stop any time soon. Car by car the members of the community, including the leaders, all left—except, of course, big Jack and little Jack. We sat and waited. Finally my dad said, "Grab your hoe, son."

"What?" I cried.

"Grab your hoe!" he said in a serious voice. "We told the man we would hoe six rows of beets. There are only about three finished. Let's go."

We got out of the truck and walked back to the beets through the mud and rain. I was furious! I kicked mud at my father and complained the entire time. I don't know how he put up with me. All I know is that it didn't stop raining, and we didn't stop hoeing until it was too dark to see. It took years for me to learn the lesson, but it finally sank in. My dad had given his word, and that was more important than staying dry or listening to a whiny fourteen-year-old. My dad knew how to work, and he knew about integrity. Eventually I learned the lesson he tried to teach me.

It is easy to feel that our teachings as parents are falling on deaf ears, but we should never stop teaching. A saying in the teaching profession goes like this: "You can only peddle fresh fish." Are we beating the same old drum of "pick up your clothes, clean your room, do your home-work, turn down your music, eat with your mouth closed, grow up, quit whining"? Or are we keeping our lessons and our families alive and fresh by laughing together, working together, trying new things together, going places together, setting goals together, learning about finances together, taking walks together, riding bicycles together, going on vacations together, talking together?

As we strive to build our relationships, it becomes eas-ier to break down barriers and express our love and affec-tion. Don't be like the man lying on the grave trying to talk to his departed loved one. Tell your loved ones now how you feel. Spend time with them. Share with them.

Building successful families, children, and lives takes time, patience, and unrelenting work. If it were easy, there would be no opportunity for growth and progress. Perhaps that is why so many people today do not want a family. If we shy away from family relationships and responsibilities because of the work, pain, and risks involved, there will be no solutions to the world's problems. Whenever God wants to change anything of significance, he sends a baby into the world.

As we take on the role of training and preparing children for the struggles of a harsh, unforgiving world, we must not tire of doing our best to help them be as good as they can be.

Chapter 6

The Power of Happiness and Peace

What are the benefits of being good? Why is it so crucial in our daily lives to live by correct and moral principles? I certainly do not have all the answers to such questions, but I know that specific powers come from being good that can come in no other way. At first, these powers may appear to be so simple that it is easy to underestimate their significance, but in the following three chapters I will discuss three powers that can enrich our lives. Each is tied to the other, and each has a specific role in helping us live a quality and productive life.

As with my list of heroes in chapter 3, the following list of powers is not complete: (1) the power to be happy and at peace amidst adversity; (2) the power to resist life-destroying influences; and (3) the power of spirituality or the ability to communicate with deity and experience deep feelings. This chapter will focus on the power of happiness and peace.

As a young teacher many years ago, I had an exceptional experience with a group of high school seniors. I left the classroom that day motivated to continue teaching and with the exhilarating feeling of walking on air. The class session had been far more than I had hoped it would be when preparing the lesson, and it appeared that each student, or at least most students, had a great learning experience and left the class desiring to learn more. Several students thanked me for the class as they departed. I made my way to the office hoping to enjoy the sweetness of the moment a little longer.

Upon entering the office, I noticed a folded three-by-five card lying on the floor. Someone had evidently slipped it under the door after class. In my pride I thought, *Wow! Someone enjoyed the class so much they had to write me a note about it!*

But after reading the neatly printed poem on the inside of the card, my heart sank as if to the gutter. The note read:

> *Every human being is trying to say*
> *Something to others,*
> *Trying to cry out,*
> *I am alive,*
> *Notice me,*
> *Speak to me,*
> *Listen to me,*
> *Confirm to me that I am*
> *Important!*
> *That I matter.*
> *"God bless us with a listening ear."*

I sat at my desk stunned, humbled beyond words. I pondered and cried. Amidst all my pride, at least one student felt unloved, unimportant, and ignored. Thoughts of the teacher-training movie *Cipher in the Snow* raced through my mind. The movie tells the true story of the death of a young student virtually unknown by any other students or teachers. He dies in a snowbank after asking his bus driver to stop and let him off the bus. The investigation of his death proves he did not die of illness but of a broken heart caused by loneliness and neglect. I wondered at the time whether this same scenario could be happening in my classroom. Didn't such things happen only to others or in the movies?

For nearly three years I searched in vain for the identity of the student who had written the note. Nothing. No one admitted to writing it. Almost three years later, a knock came at my door one day around 4:00 A.M. I put on my robe, walked to the door, and asked who it was. When I opened the door, a former student of mine, reeking of alcohol, fell into my arms, sobbing.

I helped him into the living room and called for my wife to help me. He continued to sob, eventually telling us that he had been to a party where drugs and alcohol were being abused freely and where Satan-worship was being practiced. He told us he was so scared that he came looking for a place he knew he would be safe. Finally, he calmed down.

For some reason I asked him if he had written the poem on the three-by-five card. He said, "It's about time you figured it out. I thought you never would."

"Why did you write it?" I asked. "Did you really feel you were unimportant?"

"All you ever cared about were the athletes and the cheerleaders," he replied. "You never really showed much attention to the rest of us."

"Well, then why are you here?" I asked him. "Why did you come to me for help if you felt I didn't care?"

I don't remember how he responded, but I hugged him and expressed my love for him. He stayed for a few hours, slept a little, and freshened up before returning to his apartment.

Now, many years later, he is doing quite well. We still see one another occasionally, and we love each other dearly. That experience affected me. The agony and sorrow I felt—sitting at my desk, thinking that a student in my class was hurting, and realizing that I wasn't helping in that student's time of need—haunted me. Today I am a different man and, I hope, a better teacher.

That experience and others like it helped me form a teaching philosophy based on the value of individuals and their desire to be happy. So far, this philosophy has been successful. It has evolved as I have grown in experience and tried to better understand that everyone does matter, and that all need to know they are important.

I begin each new school year by keeping in mind this simple quote by Henry David Thoreau: "I have never met a man [or woman] who is not my superior in at least one way." My philosophy is that because every human being is superior to me in at least one way—and often in many ways—they should be respected, regardless of their age, as worthwhile, significant individuals. As a teacher I want to contribute to the happiness of my students, as well as to the happiness of my family and others around me.

There must be more to our existence than simply living and dying. Unfortunately, the trouble, tragedy, heartache, and sorrow that surround us distract us from life's real purpose. I believe that happiness ought to be the object and design of our existence. It can be and will be if we pursue the path that leads to it. What is that path? It is uprightness and faithfulness to moral values and principles. It is being good! Most human beings spend their time, energy, and money striving for happiness, peace, and freedom, but these powers are best obtained by simply being good.

If one of the major desires and purposes of our lives on earth is to be happy and filled with joy, why are so many people unhappy? Why are so many downtrodden and browbeaten? Why have so many lost hope?

Perhaps these questions cannot be answered. Nevertheless, I know there is a direct relationship between our striving to be good and our ability to be happy and joyful. On several occasions after I have spoken on this subject, people have come up to me and voiced their frustration. They say, "I'm a good person who is trying to do everything I can that I believe is right, and I still feel miserable and unhappy most of the time. I don't like myself. I don't enjoy life. What you are saying just isn't true!"

There may be no quick or easy answers to all of life's difficult questions and problems. Some physical, emotional, and mental disorders (such as those caused by chemical imbalances) may be major factors in our happiness and behavior.

The reality of being human is that bad things sometimes happen to good people. Doing everything we can to live according to moral values does not mean we will be free of tragedy. One of life's great lessons is that there is opposition in everything. Opposition exists even when things are going great—especially when things are going great. Opposition is actually an exacting teacher if we are wise enough to learn from it rather than becoming bitter and giving up on life. We cannot know happiness and joy if we do not know heartache and sorrow.

Life consists of many experiences; some are not only unfortunate but completely unfair. Tragedies happen in all of our lives, and we all struggle from time to time. One key to success lies in how we deal with difficult situations. Some setbacks come as a result of our poor choices, while others come as a result of the poor choices of others. Some setbacks come because we have imperfect bodies and live in an imperfect world.

M. Scott Peck has written, "Life is difficult. This is a great truth, one of the greatest truths. It is a great truth because once we truly see this truth, we transcend it. Once we truly know that life is difficult—once we truly understand and accept it—then life is no longer difficult. Because once it is accepted, the fact that life is difficult no longer matters" (*The Road Less Traveled* [New York: Simon & Schuster, 1978], 15).

Happiness and peace do not always equate with everything in life running smoothly. Happiness and peace are powers that come from within as we live by true and virtuous principles, even amidst adversity. If we continue to be good through difficult times, we learn that God uses *broken* things to teach us some of life's greatest lessons. "It takes broken soil to produce a crop, broken clouds to give rain, broken bread to give strength. It is the broken alabaster box that gives forth perfume. . . . It is Peter, weeping bitterly, who returns to greater power than ever" (Vance Havner, quoted in *Guideposts,* October 1981, 5).

Consider the "Wayfarer's Lament," written by my teaching colleague and friend John Young:

> *O Lord, I was caught up in the raging*
> *flood, wrenched from my path and*
> *purpose, and nearly drowned time and*
> *time again.*

*I was dashed from stone to stone with
merciless force, choked with water and
tossed this way and that.*

*In pain and terror I wept for my helpless-
ness, my weakness, and called upon thee
for help. I poured out my soul with all
the energy I possessed for help, but where
wast thou?*

*I was bruised and broken and dragged for
miles in the current, unable to escape the
force of the stream. I was battered until I
had no will left even to live. I put my des-
tiny in thine hand, and where wast thou?*

*The terrors of the tide drove from me all
care for the things of my life: my possessions, my place among men, and, in the
end, even care for my life itself.*

*All strength to resist was taken from me,
all energy to strive against the waves.
And then, when I was weakened beyond
pride, beyond fear, beyond care for anything, and I simply yielded myself to
the flow, I found myself limp, and
breathless on this foreign shore.*

O Lord, where wast thou?

*My son: Thou hast traveled far, through
grief, toil, and trial. Thou standest here
naked—dispossessed of all things and
all earthly cares. Thou standest here on
sacred ground, in a new and promised
land.*

My son, I was always with thee.

I was the water!

Are the waters of life taking you to and fro and beating you against the rocky shores? Are their currents strong and powerful? Does it seem that it is impossible to change or be happy and free because you've tried before and failed? You've been unhappy so long, why try again to be otherwise? Why? Because everyone can be happy no matter how much sorrow, heartache, disappointment, or failure have come into their lives by the currents of life's teaching waters. We must live by true and correct principles, realize that life is difficult, and let the power of being good work its miracle. We must be brave as the current moves us, and that bravery comes by living the principles we discussed in the last chapter.

Some years ago I heard a college president tell the story of his father, who was dying of bone cancer. He said that his father's condition became so bad that he had to be hospitalized and placed under constant supervision. Members of the family took turns sitting with their father and grandfather. They met his various needs and tried to make his last remaining days as pleasant as possible for someone with such a painful disease. As bone cancer eats away the life of the body, it causes the bones to become brittle, leading to excruciating and almost unbearable pain. Such was the case with this man's father.

One night while the president sat with his father, the dying man gingerly crawled out of bed and knelt on the floor to pray. Instantly, the son reached down and tried to help his father back into bed. The father refused to be helped, telling his son that he needed to pray. He said he had a very important question to ask God that required him to kneel. The son responded that he was sure God could hear and answer his prayer if he was lying on his back in bed. Again the father refused. He said he must kneel. Just the act of getting out of bed and kneeling could have caused his bones to fracture, as well as other complications, but the father continued to insist that his question was so serious that it required kneeling. Finally the son asked his father what was so important that he had to kneel. The father's response was sobering:

"Son, I want to know why, when I have been good all my life, why, when I have done what I believed was right and true every day of my life, why, when I have lived my religion every day, been faithful to my family, and been honest in all my dealings with everyone, why, as this life comes to an end, why is God allowing me to suffer so miserably?" The son was stunned. He replied, "Dad, I guess you had better pray from your knees."

How would you respond to such a question? It's a tough one, isn't it? Why do people who try so hard to do what is right end up suffering as much, or even more, than those who just live for the day and do as they please, never worrying about anyone other than themselves? Perhaps the answer the father received can give us some insight into such a difficult question.

After praying, and with help from his college-president son, the father got back into bed. The son then asked if his father had received the answer he had sought. The father was somewhat reluctant to reply, but with a bit more prodding he finally said, "Yes, son, I did get an answer. I learned that God needs brave sons, and I must learn to be brave!"

What a profound lesson to learn about being happy and at peace. We must be brave! God needs brave sons and daughters. Few statements have had as much effect on my attitude and outlook on life. Whether we believe in God or not, we must learn to be brave, no matter how hard life may be or what we may have to go through to learn life's lessons.

Instead of asking, "Why me?" when something terrible happens in our lives, we need the courage and bravery to ask such questions as "What can I learn from this?" or "How can I use this experience to help others?" All difficult things give us experience and will be for our good if we do not weaken. No suffering, pain, or heartache is ever wasted if we believe that we are to be happy. Suffering intensifies our education; it enhances the development of qualities such as patience, faith, fortitude, and humility. All that we suffer and endure—especially when we endure it patiently—not only gives us experience but builds our characters and makes us more tender and charitable toward others. It is through sorrow and suffering, toil and tribulation that we gain the education we have come to class for in the school of human experience.

One of the bravest things we will ever do is learn to make wise choices and then accept responsibility for those choices. We must cease blaming others for everything that is negative, difficult, or unfair in our lives. Somehow we must break the bonds of the credit-card mentality that blankets modern society, the mentality that says "get now and pay later." We must always pay in the end no matter how long we put off the payments. If we are responsible, we will pay now rather than wait for some future date or life-altering event.

Author and speaker Stephen R. Covey speaks often of the law of the harvest, and anyone who has ever lived on a farm or tried to grow anything knows this law well. We cannot plant at the end of the summer or only feed our stock properly prior to their sale and expect an acceptable harvest. Rather, we must learn that happiness and peace come when we spend our time and energy now in goodness and obedience to law and correct principles.

An often-told story of a young Indian warrior who made a trek up a sacred mountain to commune with the spirits illustrates this point beautifully. As he climbed higher and higher up the mountain, the temperature became colder and colder. He wrapped his buckskin tightly around his neck to keep the biting cold from chilling his flesh. As he rounded a turn in the trail, there before him was a dying rattlesnake. The snake had not made it to warmer ground soon enough and was unable to crawl with precision, for the cold air made him stiff and groggy. The warrior was frightened until he realized the snake had no strength to strike. As he contemplated what to do to get around the snake, the snake spoke to him.

"Please, brave warrior, save my life. Please pick me up. Please help me get warm so that I might make it back down the mountain to my home."

The warrior responded, "If I place you in my shirt next to my skin and you receive warmth and strength you will bite me and I will die."

"No," whispered the snake. "I promise. If you will warm me and take me back down the mountain with you, I will not bite you. I give you my word."

The warrior thought for a few moments and then asked the snake, "Why should I trust you? You are a snake and you will bite me and I will die."

"No," responded the snake again. "If you will warm me and give me life I promise that I will be your friend and I will not bite you."

After contemplating some more, the young warrior decided to trust the snake. "Surely," he thought, "if I give the snake new life he will be appreciative and spare my life."

The warrior bent down and gently picked up the rattlesnake, placing it securely next to his skin under his protective buckskin. He then proceeded up the mountain to accomplish his mission. After communing with the spirits, he began his journey down the mountain. As he descended, the sun became warmer and warmer, and the chill of the high altitudes dissipated. The sun warmed his skin, and he felt life coming back into the snake. The snake soon said, "Thank you so much, my friend. We are now near my home. Please place me on the ground and I will forever be in your debt."

The warrior carefully reached into his shirt and, speaking kindly to the snake, thanked him for keeping his word and gently placed him in the dirt. Without warning, the snake coiled and struck the young warrior just above the ankle. With venom burning as it entered his bloodstream, the warrior cried out in pain and disbelief: "I helped you. I saved your life. I believed in you. How could you bite me when I was so good to you?"

The rattlesnake calmly hissed, "You knew what I was when you picked me up!"

Are we like the young warrior? Do we contemplate the result of our bad choices, or do we foolishly believe that negative results such as addiction, pain, and loss of life or limb will never happen to us? The warrior tried to blame the rattlesnake, but the snake put the responsibility where it belonged. The warrior knew what the snake was when he picked him up. He should never have believed the snake. He knew he was poisonous.

Can happiness and peace ultimately result when we ignore principles and behavior that lead to happiness and peace? We must learn to recognize—by being good—life's pitfalls, or "rattlesnakes." The power to recognize these rattlesnakes, and know when to run from them, is another power that comes from being good.

Chapter 7

Power to Run, Power to Love

For some reason I have been afraid of spiders much of my life. I know that spiders fill an important role in the food chain and that most are harmless; nevertheless, they're still creepy. I find them more tolerable as I grow older, but I still shy away from them whenever possible.

One night, while enjoying a blissful sleep, I was awakened by my wife calling my name over and over. "There's something in our bed!" she cried. "It just ran across my arm, and it's big!"

I unwillingly crawled out of bed, turned on the light, pulled back the covers, and in a somewhat irritated voice said, "Are you happy now? There's nothing in our bed. You must be having a nightmare. Please go back to sleep and quit worrying. There's nothing here but your dreams."

After turning off the light and crawling back into bed, I attempted to take advantage of a remaining hour of sleep before having to get up. A few seconds later, Melanie jumped up on the bed again.

"Honey, it just ran across my face and it felt hairy!" she called out again, frightened.

"Good grief, Melanie, you're having a nightmare!" I said, somewhat put out.

I got out of bed, turned on the light again, and pulled back the covers. We searched the entire bed. Nothing. Finally, I grabbed my pillow and, pulling it to the edge of the bed, said, "Let's just go to sleep!" Then I saw it. On the bed where my pillow had rested was a large, brown, hairy spider. It scurried so quickly that it appeared to jump to the top of the pillow, which was still in my hand. Letting go of the pillow as if it were a hot iron, I instantly leaped for the corner of the room. It's embarrassing to admit, but I yelled, "Kill it! Kill it!"

Melanie began to laugh. "I don't believe it," she said. "My big football-player husband who thinks he's so tough is afraid of a jumping spider." She then went to the kitchen and brought back a quart jar and a plate. While I was still in the corner, she carefully got the spider into the jar and placed the plate on top as a lid. With taunting motions, Melanie brought the bottle toward me with outstretched arms, trying to get a reaction. I stayed in the corner, moving my arms in karate fashion, trying to keep the jar as far away as possible. We have had many laughs over that night.

A couple weeks later Melanie and the children went to visit her parents. During the almost two weeks they were gone, life was busy and hectic for me. Needless to say, I didn't wash the dishes or clean the house. The night before their return, I decided to clean things up. As I cleared the dishes and put them in the sink to be washed, something rather large ran across the counter and hid behind the flour, sugar, and cookie jars.

Instantly, thoughts of the spider returned. Humorously, I thought this might be the spider's mother coming for revenge. In my mind I envisioned moving the jars and having a leaping spider lunge for my neck. I guess I'd seen too many movies.

I cleared a pathway to the jars, wrapped a dish towel around my hand, and prepared to smash whatever was there. I raised my towel-wrapped hand and with my other hand quickly moved a jar. A mouse immediately ran across the counter, frantically looking for an escape route. I tried to smash it with my covered hand, but it was too fast. It ran to the edge of the counter and leaped onto my T-shirt. I went crazy as it made a screeching sound and tried to get traction while moving up my chest. Trying to knock it away, I flailed my arms wildly, my hands hitting my chest in rapid motion as if I were playing a drum. Finally the mouse fell to the floor and dragged its wounded body under the refrigerator. Later that night I caught it with a trap.

The next day while driving to pick up my family, I marveled at my fears. How could it be that a grown man with children and many responsibilities was afraid of a spider and a mouse? These creatures were basically harmless and were probably more afraid of me than I was of them. There had to be a lesson somewhere. How could phobias be used for something beneficial?

What if each of us, including our children, were just as afraid of self-destructive behaviors as I am of spiders and mice? If we were, we would run from negative, life-altering behavior as we do from small, harmless creatures. Some of us wouldn't get near a jumping spider, and the thought of a snake, rat, or mouse disgusts many of us. But what happens when life-destroying drugs, relationships, videos, music, or activities present themselves? Do we run from them?

One of the most significant powers that results from being good and making right choices is the strength to avoid activities and entertainment that are contrary to our moral convictions and principles. If we have spent energy and time deciding what we will and will not do, our response to temptation will already be determined the next time temptation raises its ugly head. If we teach our children this principle, they will not have to make the same difficult decisions over and over.

Tragically, many of us choose not to run from negative, life-altering behavior, even though we have been taught right from wrong. We tell ourselves, "Nothing bad will happen to me. I'm different. I'm mature for my age. I can handle it." Those of us who think this way refuse to accept the reality that for every choice we make, there is a consequence—good or bad—that we cannot choose. Being good and staying true to our values and convictions will do more to help us run from bad choices than just about anything else.

Reading the newspaper or watching the evening news gives us a small glimpse into the tragedy that follows in the wake of decisions not to run. Daily we hear of young people and adults drinking themselves to death, gang members taking the lives of innocent people, drug deals going bad, suicide resulting from the inability to overcome addiction and depression, and abhorrent sexual crimes being fueled by pornographic profiteers. The actions of youth who are desensitized to the immorality of behaviors and lifestyles portrayed in some music, television programs, and videos capture major headlines, shatter homes, and cause countless tears. Family members are left brokenhearted, wondering where they went wrong as they see their children, brothers, sisters, and friends suffer as a result of poor decisions.

While speaking at a leadership seminar for high school student leaders and their advisers and guidance counselors, I had a sobering experience. During the seminar we discussed the importance of avoiding behaviors that can have a negative impact on our lives. After the speech several people asked me rather specific questions about some of the issues we had discussed. A guidance counselor at a local high school asked whether I had been following the murder trial of a local young man. I indicated that I had because the young defendant, Bill,* was a former student of one of my colleagues. The murder had made headlines in most major papers around the country. As the trial progressed, the local media reported on the story almost daily.

"Well," the guidance counselor said, "I was his high school guidance counselor. Shortly after his arrest I met with him in jail. We talked for some time about the entire situation. I then asked him a penetrating question: 'How did someone like you, from a strong and stable family and with a good upbringing, go from being active in school and church to skipping school, forsaking church, taking drugs, worshipping the devil, and murdering someone? How did your life take such a tragic turn in just three years?'"

Bill's unhesitating answer to the counselor floored me: "My music. I wanted to be just like my heroes I was listening to. They sang of death, drugs, violence, sex, and the occult. I wanted to know what those things were like."

A local newspaper article and Bill's words, as related by the counselor, gave insight into how this tragedy occurred:

*Not his real name.

"I'm not making any excuses because there are no excuses. . . . If you say drugs were the turning point, you've got to ask why I did drugs in the first place. You keep going back further and further looking for answers. There is no turning point. It's the whole outcome of everything that happened."

The first blemish on the portrait of Bill's life came in the first grade when the rest of the class learned to count to one hundred. "I couldn't do it," he said. "I couldn't get past nineteen. I felt completely humiliated."

Bill said one of his teachers arranged her students in order of intelligence as she perceived it. The brightest sat on the front row. "Whoever was sitting in the last row, right seat, was stupid. That was me," he said. "The problem I had was that I looked like a normal little boy and acted like a normal little boy and played like one, . . . so what is wrong with me? Why am I so flawed?"

Bill suffered from dyslexia, a relatively common reading impairment often associated with genetic defects or brain injuries. He didn't learn about his condition until he reached death row.

"I always felt lesser," he said. "Really, you just want to be like everybody else. Your whole life at that age is going to school."

When school got tougher, Bill found ways to anesthetize himself. At twelve, according to a history he gave psychologists, he was drinking. At fifteen a group of lifelong friends asked him if he wanted to try marijuana.

"The second I did, wow!" he said. "I had found my niche in life. I finally found what I was good at. I could drink and party and do drugs like nobody else."

The counselor then related how drugs had taken over Bill's life at a very early age. On the night of the murder,

Bill and his companion were high and had been listening to heavy metal. In need of money, they decided to rob a convenience store. That night during the robbery Bill murdered a woman.

The counselor concluded by asking me to share Bill's story when speaking to young people. He hoped that it might help someone. He said Bill had asked him to relate it to as many as would listen so they wouldn't end up as he did. I assured the counselor the story would be shared whenever possible. After thanking him, I walked to my car and drove home with a heavy heart. It was sickening to think that a nineteen-year-old boy had encountered and caused so much sorrow.

Not long after my discussion with Bill's counselor, Bill was convicted of first-degree murder and sentenced to die for his crime. I will never forget watching the evening news as Bill gave his final plea for mercy before the sentence was read. His hair was cut neatly, and he was dressed in a sharp-looking three-piece suit. He wept as he read a written statement. He said he had learned many lessons since the crime and that for the first time in years he could see clearly because his mind was no longer clouded by drugs and alcohol. He wanted his life to be of value to the youth of the country. He expressed a desire to help young people understand the world of drugs, the occult, and heavy-metal and punk-rock music. He didn't want the lessons he'd learned to be wasted with his execution.

After Bill finished his statement, the judge stated simply, "Your desires are admirable, and I agree that you might be able to help other young people. However, your crime is so heinous that you will die for having committed it." What a tragedy! Nineteen years old and sentenced to die.

I share Bill's story not to suggest that others who

become involved in similar behavior will become murderers; I share it to show what may eventually happen if we do not run from dangerous situations. The challenges many of us face as a result of poor choices may not be as dramatic as Bill's, but they can still bring sorrow, disappointment, and unhappiness.

Bill just wanted to fit in, even if it was as the best drug and alcohol abuser. As parents and adults, we must give youth a sense of belonging. Young people especially need a friend who will strengthen them and in whom they can confide, even if that friend is a parent, teacher, or other adult. We all need to belong. We all need someone with whom we can share our dreams, hopes, and visions without fear of feeling stupid or rejected. We all have a basic need to feel we are contributing to a family, a community, or some worthwhile cause. Otherwise we may contribute to unworthy causes.

While speaking at a banquet many years ago, I found a small piece of paper stuck in a cupcake. The words on that paper caused deep reflection. They read, "The entire sum of existence is the magic of being needed by just one person." Doesn't every human being have that desire? Most people want to be someone special.

People matter. In order to really love and build them, we must be obedient to true and correct principles. We must run from negative influences that would corrode our foundation of goodness. The power to love and the power to run are directly related to our ability to be good. But what if you are the one who feels unloved? What if you are the abused, the downtrodden, the forgotten? What if you are the one sitting on the "stupid row" in the back? What if you are the one who is made fun of or who is the brunt of every joke? How do you get others to love you?

As difficult as it may seem, you must love others first. In most cases, others will eventually love you in return. There will always be those who are so hard-hearted and self-centered that their love waxes cold. But for most, the principle is true: As you love others they will love you.

In my department each year at Christmastime, students undertake several service projects that generate thousands of dollars. Students use the funds primarily to purchase Christmas gifts for struggling single-parent families. If not for the love and concern of many wonderful young people, these families would have no Christmas presents. One of my colleagues received the following letter from a young man who had been involved in one of the many projects.

Dear Miss Rasmus' class,

I am writing this letter and having Miss Rasmus read it to you because I was extremely touched when I found out what your class was doing for this family. The reason why is because when I was nine years old my family was going through an extremely difficult year. My father had to file for bankruptcy when he lost the two pharmacies that he managed; my brother had to have surgery on his knee, shoulder, and ankle from a football injury; my sister Laura had her appendix taken out; my father had a heart attack and five bypasses from the stress of losing his stores; my sister Jana got married; my grandfather died of cancer; and I broke my leg.

After all of these occurrences in 1987, my family was very short of money. My parents were very afraid and worried what was going to happen to my family. As Christmas came upon us, my parents gathered all eight children together and told us that we were not going to have much of a Christmas that year. We all understood completely and felt very low and down.

Christmas Eve came and it was a very melancholy night. During Christmas dinner someone came over to our house—we don't know who, but when we opened the door we found three garbage bags full of presents for all my family. That was a very rare experience, for it was only one of a few times I have ever seen tears of joy in my father's eyes. That Christmas was turned from gloomy to joyous in a matter of minutes, just by the showing of love and care for my family by someone else in our greatest time of need.

That Christmas was one of the greatest and fondest Christmases of my life. I was so thankful for all the love people showed me and my family that Christmas. I am just thankful for your class's willingness to serve and love this family. When I was asked to help put Christmas lights up at people's houses [in order to raise money for others' gifts], your love and charity struck me very hard. It struck me so profoundly that I would like to donate my paycheck of Thanksgiving week to your family and cause, for I was helped, and I am sure the family you are helping is just as thankful. That is why I would appreciate your adding my check for $170 to your fund. I want to thank you for thinking of this wonderful and loving idea, for people like you are what make a child's Christmas go from sadness to joy. Thank you again.

As expressed in this young man's letter, life is often filled to capacity with challenges and hardships. But as we love others first, we can play a small part in turning their lives from sadness to joy. When part of our personal struggle comes from feeling unloved or not needed, it would be wise to forget ourselves and discover the magic of loving others.

The power to run from self-destructive and dangerous

influences is a power that each of us needs in order to find true happiness. As we reject the negative and embrace the positive, we will find the inner strength to love ourselves as well as others, even when we feel rejected or snubbed. As we master this ability, we master that which can bring us the most joy and the greatest measure of long-lasting peace.

Chapter 8

The Power of Spirituality

The word "spirituality" conjures up a wide range of feelings, attitudes, opinions, and responses, depending on an individual's upbringing, religious preference or non-preference, experience, and lifestyle. It seems that spirituality has become a lost art. People seem afraid of offending others by talking about spiritual matters in mixed circles. Others are reluctant to develop spirituality along with their mental, emotional, physical, and social talents.

I believe spirituality is the greatest of all the talents and gifts we can acquire, but it must be developed. Spirituality helps us understand our feelings. If we become past feeling, we are in trouble as individuals, families, communities, and nations. We must be able to feel or we lose the ability to care and feel compassion for others. As the old saying goes: We are not human beings trying to have a spiritual experience, we are spiritual beings trying to have a human experience.

The prolific writer and thinker C. S. Lewis made this perceptive observation: "It is a serious thing to live in a society of possible gods and goddesses, to remember that the dullest and most uninteresting person you can talk to may one day be a creature which, if you saw it now, you would be strongly tempted to worship, or else a horror and a corruption such as you now meet, if at all, only in a nightmare. All day long we are, in some degree, helping each other to one or the other of these destinations. It is in the light of these overwhelming possibilities, it is with the awe and the circumspection proper to them, that we should conduct all our dealings with one another, all friendships, all loves, all play, all politics. There are no *ordinary* people. You have never talked to a mere mortal. Nations, cultures, arts, civilizations—these are mortal, and their life is to ours as the life of a gnat. But it is immortals whom we joke with, work with, marry, snub, and exploit—immortal horrors or everlasting splendors" (*The Weight of Glory and Other Addresses* [New York: Macmillan Publishing, 1980], 18–19).

Something happens to us when we realize deep in our souls that all individuals have value and a spark of the divine within them. This realization changes people and behavior. Once we accept that people are more than mere physical or mental beings, we lose our desire to willingly injure, cheat, or lie to others. Our lives then begin to be governed by moral principles and values. Morality is not something to be hidden and swept under the carpet. The most meaningful laws in a society are moral, biblical laws. It is morally wrong to kill, rape, steal, abuse, lie, and be unfaithful. Basing our treatment of others on moral law has practical value. Obedience to moral law generates feelings of dignity and self-respect, while reducing feelings of depression and self-pity. Through obedience to moral law, we develop self-discipline and the ability to live a good life and accept even life's hardest lessons. This understanding is the basis of spirituality.

If ever there were a time in which the power to live by moral and correct principles were needed, it is now. A blanket of darkness and gloom seems to be covering the earth as never before, but it can be overcome.

To paraphrase one of my influential teachers: Corruption is rapidly expanding in every segment of our society. It is more highly organized, more cleverly disguised, and more powerfully promoted than ever before. Gangs, drug cartels, and secret organizations lusting for power, gain, and glory are flourishing. Some organizations are even seeking to overthrow the freedom of all lands, nations, and countries. Their evil influence appears to be ever on the rise (Ezra Taft Benson, "I Testify," *Ensign*, November 1988, 87).

On the other hand, goodness is also on the rise! The number of those who desire to be good and do good is growing. Light can overcome darkness. If we can learn from the past, we will not become like so many other societies that have fallen into spiritual decline and self-destruction.

Now is the time for young and old alike to stand tall, be brave, and stay true to their principles and values. Consider some statistics: In 1987 the American Medical Association reported that the three major killers of youth between ages fifteen and twenty-four were, in order, accident (60 percent of those were auto accidents, most of which were drug- or alcohol-related), homicide, and suicide. The statistics have not changed much in the past decade, but AIDS has also crept in as a major killer.

Fighting the scourge that is claiming our young people will take great moral courage, but exercising moral courage will enhance our credibility. When we act in harmony with our conscience and beliefs, we fulfill the fundamental requirement for inner peace and security.

With the power of negative influences increasing and becoming ever more organized, it is vital that we see things clearly. Without the power of spirituality—the ability to feel—it is impossible to see ourselves and our future with much clarity. Understand, however, that spirituality is not acquired suddenly. It is the result of a succession of good choices. It is the harvest of living a good life based on sound and correct principles and values.

As young people, many of us were taught the four most significant ways of getting and maintaining the vision that comes through spirituality: prayer or meditation, study of the scriptures or other writings that teach virtuous and successful living, obedience to moral law, and service to others.

1. *Prayer or meditation.* As children, many of us sat in Sunday school or other religious services and learned of the importance of prayer. What has happened to our child-like faith and acceptance of a power greater than ourselves? Have we become so sophisticated that we think we can maneuver the stormy seas of life without help from above? As we strive to be good, the power of spirituality returns us to our roots and to the simple things in life. I'm not talking about praying without sincerity or meditating because we don't have anything else to do. I'm talking about truly giving thanks and being grateful, pleading for divine guidance, asking for forgiveness, strength, courage, charity, endurance, and whatever else we need.

To illustrate this point, I share a brief story and a poem that have often brought me to my knees. One night after I gave a lecture, a man approached me and handed me a poem. He told me a story about the poem's author, whose criminal activities I had read about in the local newspaper. The author had been convicted of molesting and murdering several young boys, and he was sentenced to die by lethal injection. A few days before the execution the man who gave me the poem was called to the prison for his final visit. During that visit the prisoner asked the man, who served as his religious adviser, to share the poem with the youth of America in hopes that they wouldn't end up in a similar situation. The man then said to me, "Please, when the time is right, will you publish this poem and speak about it in order to help me carry out the author's request and to teach people the importance of prayer, regardless of their religious affiliations or beliefs?" I hope this poem, titled "The Wrong Path Chosen," helps all who read it.

I wonder where I went wrong,
In my youth and in my past.
Life's changes were quite sudden
To bring good to bad so fast.
In eagerness I started out,
Life's mysteries to explore.
My parents gave me a good life,
In foolishness I sought more.
My youth held some accomplishments,
Great was my hope to please.
My desires to serve the Lord
Brought me often to my knees.

Upon my path temptation came
Which alone, I could not escape.
Too proud to call for needed help,
I chose my dreadful fate.

My future now holds little hope
And my life is full of fear.
The sentence of death upon me
Calls hell's presence oh so near.
Deep within these prison walls
I'll spend the rest of life.
No more dreams or hopes or pleasures,
Never to have my own family or wife.

The nights are getting longer,
The days . . . yet longer still.
I need to find some inner strength
To climb my last big hill.
I pray it's not too late for me
To purge my soul from sin,
Or remove the doubt within my heart
So Heaven may let me in.
To young people I would say,
Be true! Be just! Be fair!
Follow the teachings of the Lord,
And fill your days with prayer.

We each need extra help at times in our lives and should not hesitate to seek out God and ask for needed strength.

2. *Study of the scriptures or other writings that teach virtuous and successful living.* Throughout history the old axiom that "the pen is mightier than the sword" has proven true. I do a lot of traveling and speaking, and I dislike hotel rooms. But the one advantage to being alone in a hotel room is that I can shower as long as I desire. At home, with a wife and four daughters, I have difficulty taking a long, hot shower. So when I'm traveling, I take full advantage, allowing the water to renew and relax me. Hot

showers renewing our bodies can be likened to the liberating and exhilarating experience of searching and studying words that give life, vision, and spiritual strength. The Psalmist wrote, "How sweet are thy words unto my taste! yea, sweeter than honey to my mouth! . . . Thy word is a lamp unto my feet, and a light unto my path" (Psalm 119:103, 105).

Is studying and learning sweeter to our taste than honey to our mouths? Are we learning and studying things that can guide our decision-making processes? Is our reservoir of knowledge and spiritual understanding deep enough to prevent us from being blown in every direction as a wave upon the sea? Have we become familiar enough with valuable words and teachings so that we become, as Mr. Keating tried to teach his students in the movie *Dead Poets Society,* able to allow the words of the poets and prophets to ooze from our lips like honey? Do we hear and feel the words of those speaking to us from the pages of scripture, history, and literature? Do they become a part of us? Or are they just words on a page that greet blind eyes, fall upon deaf ears, and ricochet off hardened hearts?

Another great teacher in my life once stated, "I find that when I get casual in my relationships with divinity and when it seems that no divine ear is listening and no divine voice is speaking, that I am far, far away. If I immerse myself in the scriptures the distance narrows and the spirituality returns. I find myself loving more intensely those whom I must love with all my heart and mind and strength" (*Teachings of Spencer W. Kimball*, ed. Edward L. Kimball [Salt Lake City: Bookcraft, 1982], 135). To immerse ourselves is more than mere dipping; it requires time, work, and effort.

Technology allows us to communicate at lightning

speeds, but we must not forget basic and important spiritual communication. By doing the simple things, we stay close to our spiritual roots.

3. *Obedience to moral law.* To maintain a high level of spiritual sensitivity, we must learn to run from any temptation or situation that would destroy our inner peace and contradict our moral values.

4. *Service to others.* One of the best and clearest indicators that we are progressing and becoming spiritually sensitive is the way we treat other people. Rendering service not only helps others but takes our minds off ourselves, which allows us to put our problems in perspective. By getting our minds off ourselves and working to relieve human suffering, we bring a sense of spiritual power into our lives and learn what life really is all about. A man who truly understood how to love and serve shared this wise counsel: "Be one who nurtures and builds. Be one who has an understanding and a forgiving heart, who looks for the best in people" (Marvin J. Ashton, "The Tongue Can Be a Sharp Sword," *Ensign,* May 1992, 20).

By serving people, we leave them better than we found them. By serving, we become fair with our competitors, whether in business, athletics, or elsewhere. By caring about others and seeking to meet their needs, we don't get drawn into the seemingly dominant attitude of our times—trying to win by intimidation or by undermining someone's character. Lend a hand to those who are frightened, lonely, or burdened.

If we could look into each other's heart and understand the unique challenges each of us faces, we would treat each other with more gentleness, love, patience, tolerance, and care. Isn't the essence of spirituality serving others? Does not the service of others equate with serving God? The power of spirituality that comes from being good is personified in serving others. Serving people is so important because people matter more than anything else, including possessions, honors, careers, or academic degrees.

As a young boy I dreamed of owning a Schwinn three-speed bike with the gears mounted on the handlebars just above sparkling red plastic handle grips. The bike I wanted had long, thin, plastic streamers of red, yellow, white, green, and blue hanging from the grips. The streamers had a distinct smell—just like a new Christmas doll. The bike had a two-tone red-and-white seat with a large white S in the middle, and it sported skinny tires. Hand brakes are common today, but back then they were new. I had never ridden a bike with hand brakes, and I longed to do so.

For years, each Christmas brought the hope that somehow my parents could afford my dream bike. That hope never materialized. It seemed as if I always received the same things: an orange and hardtack candy in my stocking, some underwear (I wanted boxer shorts but usually got briefs with red dots around the waistband!), socks, a pair of jeans with a button fly, some T-shirts, and a basketball. Once in a while I received some pajamas. At the time I never realized how hard my parents had worked and how much they had sacrificed to provide what they could.

Christmas changed for me years later when I was a grown man. One evening as I drove home from work, a public service announcement from the state social services agency came on the radio. The agency was asking for volunteers to provide Christmas gifts for patients at a state hospital who had no family or friends. What a great idea! Upon arriving home I ran into the house and presented the proposal to my wife. She listened patiently and then told me I was too late—she had heard the same announcement and had already called the hospital to have a patient assigned to us. We were both thrilled to have an opportunity to buy for a needy person instead of just for ourselves and our children.

The gentleman was fifty-five years old. He suffered from severe mood disorders and only needed a few items of clothing. After reading the meager list of his needs, I stood in the kitchen in disbelief. The things he needed were the things I had not appreciated as a young boy: T-shirts, socks, pajamas, and underwear. Rarely in my life had I felt more humbled. It seemed that I was being given the opportunity to make up, somewhat, for all my ingratitude as a child.

The hospital gave us strict orders not to bring food items or extra gifts. I thought, however, that a couple nice dress shirts surely couldn't hurt, so we purchased them, wrapped them, and put them with the rest of our patient's packages.

The day arrived for taking the gifts to the hospital. When we arrived we were directed to a lockdown facility, which left us a little apprehensive. I went to the steps, rang the bell, and waited for someone to open the iron-barred door. It wasn't long before a young orderly answered the door. I stated my business, gave him the patient's name, and handed him the packages. He told me that our patient was having a good day and then asked if I would like to bring my family inside so we could give him the gifts ourselves. We were led to a small dining area, and our patient, sitting in a wheelchair, was brought to meet us.

A blanket was wrapped around his legs, and he was wearing a sweatshirt. He hadn't shaved for two or three days, and crumbs from his dinner were spread around his mouth. He could not, or would not, speak.

The orderly asked him if he wanted to open the packages or have us open them for him. He didn't respond, so the orderly handed us the packages, and we began opening them one by one. As we did so, tears began streaming down the patient's cheeks. This sweet, lonely man was crying over T-shirts, socks, pajamas, and underwear with red dots around the waistband. Humility swept over me. No one said anything, but we all felt deep gratitude for the blessing of giving.

One of our young daughters began to cry and asked, "Doesn't he like our presents? Is he sad that we brought him pajamas?" We tried to explain that he was shedding tears of joy, but she was too young to understand.

As we drove home, the car was silent. When we pulled into the driveway my daughter again said she still didn't understand why the man cried if he was happy. As we again tried to explain tears of joy, we taught our children about the joy of giving. Serving others took on new meaning that day for our family.

We never saw the man again, but we have tried to do something special for others ever since, and we have all been changed as a result. Christmas is the most exciting time of the year for us. We can hardly wait to give and bless others' lives. Of course, we should be giving, blessing, and serving every day, but doing it at Christmas has a special significance. The joy I feel when serving means much more than any possession I own or desire.

Truly, spirituality and the ability to feel and be sensitive to others is a power that comes from being good. It is a power from which everyone on earth could benefit. If we all cared about each other a little more and tried a little harder to be good, the entire world would be a happier place with less sorrow and more joy.

Spirituality is not something to be feared or to shy away from. As we strive to obtain it, our lives will be more fulfilled and our hearts more at peace. I hope that as we strive to incorporate into our lives the four practices suggested in this chapter we will understand that spirituality is a vital link to all who want happiness and true freedom.

Chapter 9

Not Losing Hope

At 7:00 P.M. on October 20, 1968, a few thousand spectators still sat in the Mexico City Olympic stadium. It was cool and dark as the last of the marathon runners were carried off in exhaustion to first-aid stations. More than an hour earlier, Mamo Wolde of Ethiopia—looking as fresh as when he had started the race—powerfully crossed the finish line, the winner of the grueling 26-mile, 385-yard event.

As the remaining spectators prepared to leave, those sitting near the marathon gates suddenly were aroused by the sound of sirens going off and policemen blowing whistles. Confused, the spectators looked toward the gate. There, entering the stadium, came a lone figure wearing the colors of Tanzania. His name was John Stephen Akhwari. He was the last man to finish the marathon. His leg was bloodied and bandaged, and he grimaced with each step. He had severely injured his knee in a fall, and he hobbled painfully around the 400-meter track.

The remaining spectators arose and applauded the

courage of this man as if they were receiving the winner. Akhwari crossed the finish line and slowly walked off the field without turning to the cheering crowd.

Asked why he had not quit despite the pain and no chance of winning a medal, he said, "My country did not send me 5,000 miles to *start* the race; my country sent me to *finish* the race" (Robert D. Hales, "Behold We Count Them Happy which Endure," *Ensign,* May 1998, 76).

We are on earth not only to begin a race with mortality but to finish it. We may be bloody, bandaged, and grimacing as we approach the finish line, but as we move forward as best we can, our endurance will turn to success and our lives will not have been wasted. There is no need to take a Kevorkian exit. What the world needs is finishers who do not lose hope, get discouraged, or give up!

It is easy to lose hope if we concentrate only on our imperfections. In the King James Bible, the Greek word translated as "perfect" can also be translated as "complete, finished, fully developed." Alternative translations from the Hebrew for "perfect" are "complete, whole, having integrity." Is anyone complete, finished, whole, fully developed? In order to become perfect, we would certainly need more than one lifetime, so being perfect doesn't necessarily mean being without flaw.

As we seek to be good and improve our lives, we must not let our weaknesses discourage us or our flaws cause us to lose hope. Becoming good means becoming better not becoming perfect. It is a lifetime pursuit that involves slow, almost imperceptible growth and change. We often read or hear of people whose lives, in an instant, changed dramatically—or so it seemed. Such astonishing examples of the power to change can lift and reach even those in deepest despair. But we must be cautious as we discuss such remarkable examples. They may be real and powerful, but they are more often the exception than the rule.

For each person who changes in an instant, millions of people find the process of improvement slow and subtle. Most of us improve day by day, step by step, little realizing that we are gradually achieving our goals of self-improvement and that we are influencing others for good. We need to be concerned with the direction we are traveling not the speed at which we are traveling.

It is always helpful to look to others for examples of goodness. The following story is about a family who did not lose hope in the face of one of life's most tragic and trying circumstances. Instead, they continued to do good and live life to the fullest.

> We'd just cut the watermelons at a Sunday-school picnic, and I was laughing at the kids' antics—pretending to play harmonicas as they munched on the sweet pink slices, using the rind to make big green grins, seeing who could spit seeds the farthest. When I felt the woman's hand on my arm and saw her sympathetic, questioning eyes, I knew what she'd say before she even spoke.
>
> "You seem so happy. Really happy. How do you do it after . . . after all that's happened to you?"
>
> Again and again people ask me that same question—people who know that Louis and I had three children born with the blood disorder called Cooley's anemia. First Mary Lou, then Rosemary, then George. One after the other, they were born with it, lived with it and died of it.
>
> How can I be happy after all that's happened? Well . . .
>
> Mary Lou was born in 1955. She was our second child, born two years after our strong and healthy

daughter, Ann. At first I'd thought Mary Lou's pale skin meant she took after my side of the family. Louis and I are both of Mediterranean descent, but he's the one with the olive complexion. When I took her to the pediatrician for her three-months checkup, he asked me to set up an appointment at the hospital in New York City for testing. "She seems to be anemic," he told me.

Anemia? It didn't sound too bad; lots of people have anemia. But after Mary Lou was tested at New York Hospital's Cornell Medical Center, the doctor called Louis and me in for a consultation.

"I'm sorry to have to tell you this," the doctor said. "Your baby has *thalassemia major*." He explained that this is commonly known as Cooley's anemia, after the doctor who discovered it. A rare genetic blood disorder, it prevents the body from manufacturing hemoglobin, the part of the red blood cells that carries oxygen from the lungs to body tissues and muscles.

"It mainly affects people of Mediterranean heritage," he told us. He also said that Cornell Medical Center was headquarters for the Harold Weill Clinic, which specializes in treating children with blood diseases. Mary Lou would have to go there every two weeks for a blood transfusion.

From then on I drove my small daughter into New York City from New Jersey regularly. After a few months she seemed to get used to it. And she had company; there were 19 other children being treated for the same illness.

Louis and I wanted more children, but now we wondered.

"Don't worry," our doctor assured us, "it is very rare that this happens in a family twice."

Rosemary was born in 1959. She looked fine— bright blue eyes and fine brown hair like Mary Lou's.

But just to be certain, I quickly took her to the clinic to be examined. The doctors were noncommittal. Weeks went by. One day she'd seem perfectly normal, the next her head would be sweating. The pattern had been the same with Mary Lou. Then, when she was six months old, the doctor gently told me that Rosemary would also need regular blood transfusions.

"Why didn't you tell me before?" I whispered. "Why did you let me hope?"

He shook his head sadly. "We knew how difficult it would be for you to hear this outright. We hoped you would recognize it gradually on your own."

So now I was driving two little girls into the city. It was easy to see how much Mary Lou and Rosemary depended on the transfusions. As the time for the treatments neared, they would tire easily and become irritable. But after their hospital visit—grueling as it was—they seemed fine. In the meantime, Louis and I tried to give our three daughters a normal life with music lessons, Monopoly games and plenty of family outings.

In 1961 our son, George, was born. We had yearned for a boy and we'd been assured that the chances of our having another child with the same affliction were absolutely nil.

But from the first moment I held my little boy in my arms, I knew. Deep down, I knew. Soon I was taking George into New York along with two-year-old Rosemary and six-year-old Mary Lou.

Even so, Louis and I were grateful for four lovely children. The blood transfusions simply became a regular part of our lives, and we went on hoping that a medical breakthrough would make them unnecessary. Meanwhile we were busy with the usual family things—school activities, music lessons, outings and vacations; and the years passed.

Then came our shocking discovery.

One morning while I was waiting at the hospital, a mother of one of the other children quietly handed me a clipping from *The New York Times* headlined FATAL BLOOD DISORDER. It was about children coming to that very clinic. One sentence blazed out at me. *"They usually die before they are 20 years old."*

I couldn't believe it. I took the clipping to our doctor. "Is it true?" I asked.

"Yes," he sighed. "I'm afraid it is."

There were no drugs, no treatments, no known medical help to prevent my children's death at a young age.

For weeks Louis and I lived in a daze. His reaction was to say little and concentrate on his work as a garment designer. Mine was to cry whenever I was alone.

The children? We couldn't bring ourselves to discuss it with them, though I knew they were aware of the seriousness of their condition from talking with the other patients during their hospital visits. And then came one of those small moments, small but significant, that changes the way you see things.

I'd walked into 11-year-old Rosemary's room one evening and found her making a jeweled butterfly pin. She was already selling her work at craft shows.

"How beautiful," I said, as I watched her carefully set a rhinestone.

"Thanks, Mom," she murmured. "I'm going to earn all I can toward college."

College? She was planning on *college?*

I cleared my throat. "Uh . . . what are you planning to study, hon?"

She looked up, eyes shining. "Nursing, Mom. I

want to be like those nice women at the hospital who help me."

She turned back to her work and I walked slowly out of the room, trying to take it all in. Rosemary was *not* thinking about death; she was focusing on life.

At Thanksgiving one of her teachers phoned me. The class had been asked to write about what they were most thankful for. The answers were the usual ones about home, parents and food. The teacher's voice trembled. "I thought you'd like to hear Rosemary's answer: 'I thank God for my good health.'"

Good health? How could she write that? And then I remembered the other children Rosemary saw on her hospital visits, the ones with amputations or suffering from cancer. But Rosemary could walk . . . go to school . . . skip rope.

Rosemary had filled our house with scripture plaques that she made herself. In her own room she'd hung the one that said: *This is the day which the Lord has made; let us rejoice and be glad in it* (Psalm 118:24 RSV).

That Thanksgiving I looked around me. I saw that our house was not a house of shadows and sorrow; our children filled it with cheerfulness and bustling activity. Mary Lou's piano music rang through the rooms as she practiced for a recital. Rosemary busily crafted jewelry and wall plaques. Little George had an extensive rock collection; he was already talking about becoming a geologist. Slowly I began to see that my children, all of them, were rejoicing in life.

On July 4, 1969, Rosemary, now 12, was in the hospital with a minor cardiac problem, a side effect of Cooley's. "You seem better, honey," I said to her that night as I leaned down to kiss her good-bye. "I'll be back early in the morning."

Just after I got home, the telephone rang. Rosemary was gone. "Peacefully," the hospital said.

We mourned. Mary Lou and George had known their lives would be short, but now, with Rosemary gone, they were forced to face that fact head-on. Mary Lou, four years older than Rosemary, began carefully tending her sister's grave. I knew that she must be contemplating her own death. And yet, I watched carefully as she took up the business of her life with a new vitality. She began making the honor roll in high school and was very popular. And she made a suggestion that gave new direction to our lives.

Louis and I had been taking our children on more and more excursions, including a week's vacation in the Pennsylvania mountains. Soon after that trip, Mary Lou returned from her hospital visit in a thoughtful frame of mind.

"Mom," she said, "when I told the kids at the clinic about our visit to the Poconos, most of them said they'd never been to a place like that. Could we find a way to take them with us next time?"

"Of course we can," I said, hugging her. Suddenly we had a project. Right away I started organizing a volunteer group to take the other children on trips. We held bake sales and candy sales and raised enough money for an excursion to Mount Airy Lodge in the Poconos. Most of the children had never been together outside the hospital. How wonderful it was to see them laughing and having a good time away from the sting of needles, transfusions and spinal taps. We found ways to raise funds to see a Broadway play and even to visit Disney World.

In 1973 Mary Lou graduated from high school as a member of the National Honor Society. She had undergone surgery for removal of her spleen, so she had worked extra hard for these honors. In the fall, she entered William Paterson College as a fine-arts major. Soon she made the dean's list. She worked part time in a TV repair shop, and her civic activities—everything from collecting for charities to volunteer work—put her in touch with almost everyone in town.

The following year she volunteered to participate in an experimental drug program for the treatment of Cooley's anemia. It took a lot out of her, and she had to be hospitalized for three weeks. "But if it helps other kids, it's worth it," she said.

Mary Lou was 19 that Christmas of 1974. In January, our Christmas tree was still standing in the living room. For some reason I just couldn't take it down.

On January 20th, it snowed heavily, keeping all of us at home. Mary Lou practiced her piano in the morning, but she was very tired. "I think I'll rest for a while," she said as she went up to bed. Later I brought her some lunch.

"Oh, this soup is so *good!*" she exclaimed. Then the light went out of her eyes and she fell back on her pillow.

Mary Lou's funeral was one of the largest ever seen in West Paterson. Louis and I had no idea that she had had so many friends. The mayor and the entire city council were there. In the words of the Cooley's volunteer group who honored her, she had been "a very special girl who lived and understood life better in her 19 years than most of us could possibly hope to if we lived to be 100."

Later, as a cold February rain battered our living-room window, I sat alone, thinking about this radiant daughter. Sighing, I leaned back, staring at the wall. In my line of sight were three of the scripture plaques her sister Rosemary had made for us. *I will never leave thee, nor forsake thee* (Hebrews 13:5). *Casting all your care upon him; for he careth for you* (1 Peter 5:7). *Do not be anxious about tomorrow* (Matthew 6:34 RSV).

The words wavered in my vision, then cleared. I got up immediately and began preparing dinner for my family.

Our oldest daughter, Ann, was involved in her career, and George, a typically noisy teenager, kept our house lively. His friends came and went, and the telephone rang constantly. He dated and had an after-school job at a local restaurant. We continued to take the Cooley's children on trips and have get-togethers.

George graduated from high school and went on to Paterson College, where he threw himself into a full schedule of activities. He went on working part time at the restaurant, and the summer he was 19 he bought a Chevrolet Monza sports car—shiny black with fire-engine-red trim. It was a young man's dream—and always full of his friends. He kept it in showroom shape.

That's why, on the night of September 20, I knew something was wrong. George came home from a date, and after he went to bed I happened to notice that his Monza was pulled into the garage at a careless angle. Always before he'd aligned it so neat and straight.

The next morning he stayed home from school. "Mom," he said. "I just can't make it anymore. I'm so tired."

Louis and I took him for a long ride that night, knowing the moving car's hum and rhythm would help him doze off. When we got back to the house, he sank down on the couch. "I know I'm going, Mom," he said wearily. He looked up at me with concern. "Promise me you won't cry? You know where I'll be."

"No, Georgie, I won't cry."

My son smiled, shook his head and lay back, eyes closed. Then he took a deep breath and was gone.

Mary Lou.

Rosemary.

George.

. . . And so, again and again, people ask that question, "How can you be happy after all that's happened?"

I'll tell you how.

My children understood that life is a holy gift from our Creator. They loved each day they were given, and their enjoyment and gratitude were like sunlight, warming and brightening our time together. In the face of early death, they embraced life. If they loved life as much as they did, honoring it, reaching out to soothe their stricken friends, using their days creatively, am *I* to love life any less?

No! I will not dishonor God—or my children—with gloom and self-pity. I embrace life as they embraced it, and I shall rejoice and be glad in it! (Mary Manachi, "Loving Life Enough," *Guideposts,* February 1985, 40–44; reprinted with permission).

Louis and Mary did not lose hope, and they did not drop out of the race. They were finishers! They learned the lesson that every human being needs to learn: Life may be harsh, mean, and unfair, but it is a gift through which we progress one step at a time.

The reality of being human is that we all suffer pain and sorrow. But the joy of rejoicing in life and not losing hope can be equal to the sorrow, suffering, and pain. We could not know deep and abiding joy and happiness if life did not teach us so much about sorrow. It is the suffering that allows us to recognize the joy, provided we do not lose hope and quit. Remember, God did not send us to earth merely to start the race; he sent us to finish it.

Chapter 10

Seize the Day

In May 1970 something happened in my teenage life that taught me a valuable lesson about living each day as if it were my last and about treating others as if each day were their last.

My older brother is a car dealer, and he was already in the car business when I reached the magical age of sixteen and could start driving. He purchased a 1962 white Cadillac convertible with power *everything* for my sister and me. We were supposed to share it, but I managed to take ownership from the beginning. My friends and I called the car the "White Stallion." It was so long and spacious, we felt invincible. We would jump into it without opening the doors, and the girls we tried to impress thought we were pretty cool.

One afternoon in May my friend Taylor Manning and I drove the White Stallion up a local canyon to the hometown ski resort. Just for fun, we drove with the top down. As 3:00 P.M. approached we headed back so I would not be late for my job as a cook at a local fast-food restaurant.

When we came out of the mouth of the canyon, we decided to take a different way home. That little decision forever changed the way I look at life.

As we came out of the canyon we were traveling approximately seventy miles per hour, which was the speed limit. The oncoming traffic was thick, but we paid little attention to it as we glided effortlessly down the highway. It wasn't long before we noticed a group of boys standing at the roadside. We found out later that they were a Little League baseball team on their way home from practice. They stood waiting for a break in the traffic so they could cross the road.

We slowed down a little and watched them closely. Two of the boys, seeing a brief break in the traffic of the oncoming lane but failing to look in our direction, bolted into the street right in front of us. It all happened in an instant. I slammed my foot on the brakes and made some quick judgments. I concluded in a split second that if I continued straight ahead, I would hit the two ten-year-olds; if I veered to the right, I would hit several boys. The only escape from tragedy was to the left, into the lane of oncoming traffic. I made my decision and quickly turned the screeching car to the left. The two boys heard the screaming of the tires on the pavement and looked up. One stopped and jumped back, out of the way; the other jumped forward. The car's front end missed him, but we plunged off the road into a weed-filled patch of field, tipped onto the passenger-side door, and skidded through the field into a ditch. Miraculously, the car didn't roll and crush us. We had turned 180 degrees, coming to a stop facing the direction from which we had come. When the dust settled and we realized the Cadillac was a total loss, we were angry. "Let's go get them!" one of us said.

We jumped from the car to find an unexpected horror. We thought we had missed both boys, but we hadn't. The boy who had jumped forward had been hit by the back end of our car and knocked about 150 feet down the road. When Taylor and I reached him, we found an ugly scene. He had a compound fracture in one leg that was bleeding profusely. The large fin just above the Cadillac's taillight had apparently hit him in the head. The impact had caused a massive head wound from one ear across his forehead to his temple, ripping his scalp away from the skull. His skin and clothes were torn off one side of his mangled body as he skidded across the asphalt.

I quickly applied a tourniquet using my belt, put his scalp back in place, and covered his head with my shirt, trying to stop the bleeding. As the boy went into shock, only one thought came to my mind: *Pray*! So I did.

People came from all around to help us, and we were able to stop the boy's bleeding. As we waited for the ambulance, some of his friends, caught up in the emotion of the moment, yelled, "You killed Michael! You killed Michael! You crazy drunken driver. You killed Michael!" I'll never forget those words as long as I live. They pierced me to the core. Had I killed him? Only time would tell. For the moment, the screams of little boys rang loudly in my ears. "You killed him! You crazy drunken driver!"

What if I *had* been drinking? What if I had been using drugs? My life would have been dashed to pieces just as surely as Michael's little body had been dashed to pieces. The highway patrolman arrived and took over first aid. Then the ambulance came and rushed Michael to a local hospital.

Other ambulances soon arrived. They had come to help the people in a car that had crashed trying to avoid hitting us. The car, filled with a troop of Cub Scouts, had driven off the highway to avoid a head-on collision with our car, and some of the boys were injured. It was a nightmare!

As Taylor and I walked to the patrol car with the officer, he said, "Boys, I sure hope we don't find any drugs or alcohol in the car or in your bloodstreams. That boy probably will not make it."

I sobbed through my tears, "Sir, I don't do drugs! I don't drink! I haven't had anything!" My sobs fell on deaf ears. As we walked toward the officer's car, my eyes caught sight of a baseball glove and a pair of baseball shoes lying in the road. Michael had been hit so hard that the impact had knocked him right out of his shoes. They were still tied in little bows, lying on the pavement in the spot where his feet had left them. A sick feeling swept over me. "I killed him!" I said to myself, continuing to weep.

Taylor and I went through all the sobriety tests. Though we had not been drinking or doing drugs, we were embarrassed by people slowly driving by, gazing at us.

When I left the house that day at 8:00 A.M., I had no way of knowing that two ten-year-old boys would dart in front of my car later that afternoon. What if we had been partying before leaving for home? What if Taylor and I had tried our first drinks that day in May? No one knows the future; no one knows when zero hour will arrive.

We finally made our way to the hospital emergency room to see if Michael was going to recover. As we walked in we saw a tall, distinguished-looking man with his arms around a crying woman.

The highway patrolman introduced us to the couple, Michael's parents. I fell into the big man's arms and cried for him to forgive me. He told me that the accident had been explained to him. He understood that it wasn't my fault and that I had done the only thing that I could have done. He assured me there would be no lawsuit. Despite Michael's life-threatening injuries, his father felt confident his son would be fine and that there was no need for me to worry.

Michael did live. Many days in the following months found me at the hospital visiting him after he had undergone several hours of surgery to repair his broken little body. It took time for him to heal, but today, many years later, it is difficult to tell he ever experienced such trauma.

I learned that spring day how precious and fragile life really is. I learned that one simple decision can alter an entire life and future. I learned how the kindness of one good man like Michael's father can influence a sixteen-year-old boy to want to be compassionate when others make mistakes. I learned that we can never say that our lives are insignificant and that it doesn't matter how we choose to live. It does matter! It matters for good or for bad. Our lives are not our own. We are individuals and have our independence, but everything we do affects someone else.

Each of us has only one life, but some of us behave as if we believed we were cats with nine lives. At times we live on the edge, giving little thought to the fact that at any instant we could lay our bodies down and depart this life. We eat, we drink, we make merry, not realizing that our loved ones and friends could die or be taken from us at any time. As John Lennon and Paul McCartney once wrote, "Life is very short, and there's no time for fussing and fighting, my friend."

We dare not live our lives without taking advantage of each and every day. We must seize the day! We must live and love each day as if it were our last. This is the essence of being good and doing good. We should never wait until tomorrow to make things right. There may be no tomorrow.

A great teacher taught: "Mend a quarrel. Seek out a forgotten friend. Dismiss suspicion and replace it with trust. Write a letter. Give a soft answer. Encourage youth. Manifest your loyalty in word and deed. Keep a promise. Forgo a grudge. Forgive an enemy. Apologize. Try to understand. Examine your demands on others. Think first of someone else. Be kind. Be gentle. Laugh a little more. Express your gratitude. Welcome a stranger. Gladden the heart of a child. Take pleasure in the beauty and wonder of the earth. Speak your love and then speak it again" (Howard W. Hunter, in "First Presidency Extols Meaning of Christmas," *Ensign*, February 1995, 77).

How we live today does make a difference. By being good and living by our moral compass, we can destroy a whole lot of wickedness in our world. We can begin changing and improving today. And we can finish. Let us replace our fear with faith—faith in a happy and bright future, faith in people, and faith in the good in the world. By being good, we can accomplish what King Arthur tried to accomplish in the movie *Camelot:* "Might for right. Right for right. Justice for all."

We can leave our children and grandchildren a legacy. We can leave them with stories they can tell and retell that will teach them to be as good as they desire to be.

On the morning of a great battle after the peace and happiness of Camelot had been destroyed by lying, deceit, and dissension, King Arthur found a young boy who wanted to join the battle. Armed with nothing but a small bow and a quiver of arrows, the boy told King Arthur that he had stowed away on a ship in order to come to Camelot and become a knight of the Round Table. The boy's name was

Thomas of Warwick. When Arthur asked Thomas why he had come to the battle, Thomas replied, "I intend to be a Knight."

"A Knight . . . ?" Arthur questioned.

"Yes, Milord. Of the Round Table."

Arthur then asked the boy several difficult questions about where he had learned about becoming a knight. The boy sheepishly confessed that he had never seen a knight until he had stowed away. "I only know *of* them. The stories people tell."

Arthur then asked, "From the stories people tell you wish to be a Knight?"

"I know everything, Milord. Might for right! Right for right! Justice for all!" the boy answered.

Arthur then began to remember and recall the glory of Camelot. He took out Excalibur, his sword, and knighted the boy Sir Thomas of Warwick. He then commanded Thomas to run behind enemy lines, return home, and live to tell people about the glory of Camelot and what had been tried and achieved.

Arthur's servant, Pellinor, then reminded Arthur that he must lead his men to battle. Arthur's reply to Pellinor is my final message about being good. Arthur took the boy by the shoulders and said to Pellinor, "I've won my battle, Pelly. Here's my victory!"

His victory? Just one boy. One good, obedient boy who wanted to fulfill the commandment of his king and tell others what can happen when people strive to be good.

Arthur cried out to Pellinor, "What we did will be remembered. . . . Now, run, Sir Tom! Behind the lines!"

Pellinor then asked, "Who is that?"

Arthur's response is classic: "One of what we all are, Pelly. Less than a drop in the great blue motion of the sunlit sea. But it seems some of the drops sparkle, Pelly! Some of them do sparkle!"

Arthur then cried out to the boy, hoping he would carry on the dream of the goodness of Camelot: "Run, boy!" (Alan Jay Lerner, *Camelot* [New York: Random House, 1961], 112–15).

As we run, some of us will sparkle. Yes, we will sparkle!

Index

Index

Index

Marriage: myths about, 52; challenges of, 52–55
McCartney, Paul, 113
McGwire, Mark, 46
Meditation, 88–90
Memorial Day, 22, 49–50
Mexico City Olympic stadium, 97
Moral Compass, The, 38–40
Morality, 86–88
Mothers: pioneer, 11–12; love of, 48
Mother Teresa: wall hanging of, 1–2; was good anyway, 3–4; as a heroine, 34–35; relieved suffering, 35
Mourning, 50
Mouse, story of, 75
Multiple sclerosis, 54
Murder, 77–80, 89–90
Music, 77–79

Names, honoring, 25

Obedience, 69, 86, 91–95
Occult, 77, 79
Olympics, 32–34, 97–98
Opposition. *See* Adversity

Parents: and interruptions, 44–48; should teach children to work, 51–52, 56–58
Patience, 57, 68, 92
Paul, the apostle, 3
Peace, 59–60, 69, 71
Peck, M. Scott, on difficulty of life, 64
Pellinor, 115–16
Perfection, 98
Philippines, 22
Phobias, 73–75
Pioneers, 11–12
Pond, Abigail A., 38
Pond, Harriet M., 38
Pond, Laura Jane, 38
Pond, Lyman, 38
Pond, Maria, 38
Pond, Stillman, 37–38

Prayer: and families, 51; and adversity, 66–67; and spirituality, 88–90
Pride, 60
Prisoner, story of, 77–80, 89–90
Punk-rock music, 79

Rail journey, analogy of, 52
Rasmus, Miss, 81–82
Rattlesnake, story of, 69–70
Reed, Donna, 30

Sacrifice, 54
Scripture study, 90–92
Self-discipline, 86
Self-esteem, 45
Self-respect, 86
Self-righteousness, 24–25
Sodom and Gomorrah, 4
Special Olympics, 32–34
Spiders, story of, 73–75
Spirituality, 85–96
Stewart, Jimmy, 30
Students, 35–37, 41–43, 59–62
Studying, 90–92
Suffering, 68
Swabia, 39

Talledega (ship), 22–24
Tanzania, 97
Teaching, 41–42, 59–62
Temptation, 76
Thalassemia major, 100
Thomas of Warwick, 115–16
Thoreau, Henry David, on individual worth, 62
Tocqueville, Alexis de, on America, 24
Tolerance, 52, 92
Tolkien, J. R. R., on changing our world, 4

Values, 32, 62–63, 87

Walk (ship), 22–24
"Wayfarer's Lament," 64–65
Weinsberg, wives of, 38–40

Index

About the Author

Jack R. Christianson played football for Dixie College, where he was an all-conference quarterback, and for Weber State College, where he was named the Outstanding Student in the College of Education and in the College of Health, Physical Education, and Recreation. After graduating from Weber State with a degree in English, he earned a master's degree at Brigham Young University in educational administration.

For more than twenty years, Jack has taught college and high school students—both in the classroom and on the football field. A popular speaker, he has lectured throughout the United States and Canada. He has written several books and produced numerous talks on tape. He actively serves his community and church, harbors a passion for raising dogs, and enjoys the outdoors.

Jack and his wife, Melanie, are the parents of four daughters.